To Be Honest

To Be Honest

JANET FIFE

Foreword by Nigel Forde

daybreak
London

First published in 1993 by
Daybreak
Darton, Longman and Todd Ltd
1 Spencer Court
140–142 Wandsworth High Street
London SW18 4JJ

ISBN 0–232–52013–5

A catalogue record for this book is available
from the British Library

Unless otherwise indicated Scripture quotations are taken from the
New Jerusalem Bible, published and copyright 1985 by Darton,
Longman and Todd Ltd and Doubleday & Co Inc and used by
permission of the publishers. The lyrics from the songs 'That's Me
in the Corner' and 'Many Times I've Been Smiling', performed by
Adrian Snell and written by Phil Thomson, are copyright 1979
Thankyou Music, P.O. Box 75, Eastbourne, East Sussex, BN23
6NW, and used by permission. The poem by Nigel Forde
'Insufferable, The Little Children' from *Fluffy Dice* is used by
permission of Robson Books Ltd. The lyrics from 'I Still Haven't
Found What I'm Looking For' (U2) by Paul Hewson, Dave Evans,
Larry Mullen and Adam Clayton are copyright 1986 Blue Mountain
Music Ltd and used by permission. Thanks are also due to Methuen
London for permission to quote from *Families and How to Survive
Them* by John Cleese and Robin Skynner.

Phototypeset by Intype, London
Printed and bound in Great Britain by
Page Bros, Norwich

For Gordon, Tommie,
Barbara, and Sister Hilda
who have helped me find
and live with
the truth of myself
within the love of God
Father, Son, and Holy Spirit.

Contents

Contents

Foreword

'Axioms in philosophy', said the poet Keats, 'are not axioms until they are proved upon our pulses'. Or, in other words, any theory or dogma has to be lived before it can be fully understood. The incarnation, if you like to look at it that way, is an earnest of God's honesty towards his creation: he himself has lived as a man under his own laws and understands our experience from the inside.

In a similar way, Janet Fife's call to honesty is a call to a truth that she has discovered for herself, not just a useful set of ground rules which she delivers from a distance. She looks at the mental and spiritual ruts that we get into and shows, not just by scriptural authority but through the experiences of herself and others, how the fruitfulness and clarity of the Christian life depends not on unthought-out principles or unquestioning acceptance of the apparently reasonable, but on unflinching truth and honesty.

What is particularly refreshing about her approach is that it does not continually blame us, the individual readers, for a lifetime of wrong-headedness. There is that element, of course, for 'all have sinned and fallen short of the glory of God', but this book dares go further and points out how the Church itself – the preachers, teachers, hymn writers and worship leaders – can also, and often for very good motives, promote 'correct behaviour' above complete honesty.

She makes all of us, whatever our role in the church family, re-examine our own experience, motivation and presuppositions. Of course, we all intend good, but good intentions are not enough. What, she asks, is 'good witness' – and the answers she finds are revealing. Where does Faith turn into hypocrisy? How manipulative are evangelists? And how truthful are the desires we so easily express in hymns, songs and prayers? These are important questions, for whatsoever a man soweth. . .

There is, for instance, one line in a well-used song, that I have never allowed myself to sing, and, while stolidly not singing it, have wondered whether the ecstatic voices around me knew what they were asking for with 'let my flesh life melt away'. God gave me my flesh, and I love it. When I no longer want to hear Bach or birdsong, no longer want to smell wallflowers or bonfires, no longer want to trudge through snow or sit by a blazing fire, drink wine, eat food, soak in a bath, read poetry or write it, then I promise I'll sing it. But I don't expect to in this life or expect I'll need to in the next.

And you?

I am tempted to point out more passages and cry 'Look, look!' But I shall content myself with adding one story of my own.

While on tour with a production of 'St John's Gospel' I returned with the rest of the cast to the Christian centre where we were staying; we were all weary and longing for some tea and a bed. A mission meeting for children was drawing to a close and I was called over by an aggressively charismatic young man 'to pray with this young girl who has just given her life to the Lord'. It may be that daily contact with the complete Gospel had sharpened my spiritual awareness; it may be that he was just stupid and insensitive. He laid his hand on the head of the girl who was about ten or eleven years old. 'Can you feel that warmth spreading inside you?' he demanded. 'Can you feel your heart lifting? Can you? Can you?' She, completely bewildered, probably slightly frightened, nodded without looking at him. 'That's the Holy Spirit!' he said. 'That proves you're a Christian!'

It was obvious that she felt nothing, that he didn't know that, and that she would say anything to get away from this confusion. What should have been the foundation of her Christian life was a lie. Because she hadn't felt what she was told she ought to have felt must have confirmed to her that everything that had happened that evening was a fake. And God was very likely a fake too. What a complete waste of time. No, worse than that. And all because nobody wanted to lose face. Nobody was able to be honest.

Quite a number of Christian books are merely recycled pieties. This one is not. Read it carefully. It's worth it.

Nigel Forde
York 1993

Acknowledgements

My thanks go to Geoff Howard, Jan Irving, Sister Hilda and Geraldine Casswell, who read and gave advice on all or part of the manuscript. Thanks also to the people of St Michael-le-Belfrey and St Thomas, Pendleton, who allowed me to thrash out my ideas in sermons preached to them. Finally, thanks to all those who have prayed for me, supported me, and generally put up with me while I was working on this book.

Preface

Some years ago I underwent a series of counselling sessions with my vicar, a skilled and sensitive man. After several sessions it became clear to both of us that there was something in myself that I was refusing to acknowledge. I did not know what it was, except that it was a memory so painful that I had so far been unable to face up to it. And I knew that now I had a choice: I could choose to face the painful truth, with Gordon's help, and allow God to deal with it. Or I could turn away and keep it buried. I would not have to face the pain of exposure, but I would not find healing either. That, as Gordon saw it, was the issue: 'Do we believe in healing, or don't we?' I was not sure that I did – not to that extent!

I went away and spent the next week wrestling with the decision: would I run away from the truth, or face it? I desperately wanted to run away. Yet again and again a Bible verse resounded through my mind like a promise: 'You will know the truth, and the truth will set you free' (John 8:32, *NIV*). I assumed this to mean that the thing I was suppressing was not as bad as I feared, and that allowing it into my consciousness would be a relief. Reassured, I went ahead with the counselling. The truth did emerge, gradually, from where I had buried it deep in my memory — and it was *worse* than I had imagined. Added to the pain of my self-discovery was anger at God. He had tricked me! He had led me to believe this wouldn't be so bad, and it was *hell!* But as the weeks went by I found I was indeed being healed. God was moving in the darkest recesses of my mind and my heart, and the pain was growing less. His love was reaching me where I most needed it.

It was several years before I could look back and say with genuine gratitude, 'I know the truth, and the truth has set me free.' I was free not because the truth had turned out to be pleasant, but because I had found that God could heal the worst of my pain, my shame, my fear. He could reverse the destructive patterns of a lifetime. His light could overcome my darkness. *His goodness was stronger than the worst that I could do or that could be done to me.*

We human beings instinctively hide from truth — the truth about ourselves, our world, our God. So often the truth hurts. It makes us feel small, guilty, insecure. Yet God *is* truth, and in the degree that we turn away from truth of any sort we are turning away from God. But God is also love, and so it is in facing the truth which hurts that we experience the depth of the love of God. In God love and truth meet, and in God we can face all truths without fear.

It is in that confidence that I write this book. I do not write it confident in myself as a truthful person, for I know that I am not. I am often dismayed at my capacity for self-deception and my willingness to deceive others. But the best teachers are often the ones who have found learning difficult and can understand the struggles of their pupils. In the same way I, who had and still have such a struggle to be honest, may be able to help others who also struggle. With God's help we *will* know the truth, and the truth will set us free.

1

Truth from the Heart

How to understand it all! How to understand the deceptions she had been thus practising on herself, and living under! The blunders, the blindness of her own head and heart! . . . To understand, thoroughly understand her own heart, was the first endeavour. [1]

Teresa of Avila, the sixteenth-century Spanish saint, is said to have been making a long and arduous journey when she found her way blocked by floods. She and her weary party were faced with a lengthy detour in bad weather. The holy woman lifted her eyes to heaven and exclaimed, 'If this is the way you treat your friends, Lord, no wonder you have so few!'

How often have you been angry with God? What do you do about it when you are? Do you tell him, as Teresa did? Or do you pretend to yourself and everyone else that things are fine, that you're still praising the Lord, that your halo is firmly in place?

Maybe the very idea of being angry at God seems blasphemous. Ironically, such anger often springs from faith, not from lack of faith. If we believe that God loves us and that he can do all things, we may find it difficult to accept that at times he appears to let us down. It does no good to try to hide what we really feel or think out of a false sense of reverence. God knows what is in our hearts, whether we admit it or not. But if we try to conceal our inner selves from God, he cannot draw near to us and we will drift farther away from him. The unacknowledged feelings become a barrier between him and us. A middle-aged matron once told me, 'I've been angry with God for twelve years, but I haven't told him. I've just shut him out.' How sad; but haven't we all done it? The very idea of being angry with God is too much to cope with for many of us; yet anger is a part of being human. And in our relationship with God, as in all other relationships, anger that has not been admitted and dealt with will eventually cause a breakdown in communication.

By contrast, the psalmists are bold to express the truth about what they feel even when they know it is not the truth about the situation. When they do so God meets them, and intimacy and hope are restored. In Psalm 73, for example, the psalmist expresses bitter resentment that the wicked seem to prosper more than the righteous:

> I envied the arrogant when I saw the prosperity of the
>   wicked.
> They have no struggles. . .
> Surely in vain have I kept my heart pure;
> in vain have I washed my hands in innocence.
> All day long I have been plagued;
> I have been punished every morning.
>
> (Ps. 73:3–4, 13–14, *NIV*)

Having expressed his frustration he begins to look at the problem from God's perspective, and comes to realize that his relationship with God and certainty of future glory are worth far more than the worldly wealth of the wicked. By contrast, Jesus tells the story of an elder brother who has the same problem, envy; he is jealous of what he sees as the preferential treatment his younger brother is getting. But he harbours his grudge for years without speaking of it, thereby poisoning their relationship and depriving himself of much that he could have enjoyed. Often we have to face up to the negative in order to get to the positive.

God wants truthfulness from us, however painful it may be, and he will honour it. 'The Lord detests lying lips, but he delights in men who are truthful' (Prov. 12:22, *NIV*). The people he draws nearest to himself are those who are prepared to be utterly honest: 'Who may dwell in your sanctuary? He . . . who speaks the truth from his heart' (Ps. 15:1–2, *NIV*). And truth here does not refer only to being honest when asked why we came in late on Saturday night, or whether we have finished that report the boss wanted. God wants a much more radical honesty; a truthfulness about who we are. He likes people who do not cover up their real selves. Throughout the Gospels, one of Jesus' most startling traits is his impatience with hypocrisy and false appearances. He often bypassed people's facades to get at what really made them tick. On the other hand, he responded well when people were truly themselves, even when they were unconventional or mistaken. When Nathanael was first asked to meet Jesus, he was blunt to the point of rudeness: 'Nazareth! Can anything good come from there?' But he expressed his scepticism honestly, and, astonishingly, Jesus respected that: 'Here is a true Israelite, in whom there is nothing false' (John 1:44–51, *NIV*).

However out of line we may think we are, it is important to be honest about our reactions and not bottle them up:

> If we claim to be without sin, we deceive ourselves and
> the truth is not in us. If we confess our sins, he is
> faithful and just and will forgive us our sins and purify
> us from all unrighteousness. (1 John 1:8–9, *NIV*)

If we bring something into the light we can get rid of it
and move on — otherwise we are stuck with it. We can
hold up our own growth and spiritual development for
years by refusing to face up to what is wrong in ourselves.

That is why the psalmists and other biblical writers are
so amazingly honest in expressing the full range of human
emotions. They don't try to deny their anger, their envy,
their despair, or even their desire for revenge. But having
owned up to those feelings, they can move on to express
faith and renewed hope in God's love and purpose for
them.

The wonder of it is that God accepts us exactly as we
are, and is always ready to forgive us and to cleanse us
from everything that is wrong. But he won't accept our
pretence to be something we're not, our efforts to cover
up the turmoil inside. He is offended and saddened by
our attempts to appear nicer and holier than we actually
are. He wants us to draw near to him just as we are, so
that we can know the full extent of his love for us.

I first began to learn this lesson some years ago. I
had grown up in the USA, among fundamentalists who
preached the victorious Christian life. Jesus was the
answer to all human problems — he could deal with our
sins and our weaknesses. And he did so as soon as we
were converted; to become a Christian was to put the old
nature and the old life completely behind us. We regularly
heard wonderful stories of how people changed overnight, how old temptations and failings had gone for ever.

Moreover, it was the duty of every Christian to act in such a way that the world would know Christians were 'different', that Jesus had solved our problems. Being a 'good witness' meant being cheery and positive at all times, especially in trying circumstances. Hadn't Jesus said, 'Be of good cheer, I have overcome the world' (John 16:33, *RSV*)?

No doubt it was not really presented quite as simply as this. Perhaps people did admit to having problems, to being not quite perfect yet. If so, as a child and then as an adolescent I was unaware of it. Nor was I encouraged at home to express my emotions. I grew up with the belief that it was not 'Christian' to struggle with jealousy, hatred, depression, or anger — so of course I never did! I repressed all negative feelings to such an extent that until I was 22 I honestly believed I was never angry. Then the bottom dropped out of my world.

My parents and I had returned to England two and a half years before, and I was studying for a degree. That last year at university the world seemed to collapse around me. I was facing my university finals, my parents had returned to the States, and my two closest friends had left the university. I felt isolated and alone in what was in many ways a strange country to me. I began having severe migraines which did not respond to treatment, and sometimes disabled me for days. I also developed a cyst which my doctor thought might need surgery. It later disappeared spontaneously, but all through that last year I was facing the threat of an operation.

In addition, my studies were raising doubts about my perceptions of reality. I learned that many issues were not simple and clear-cut but complex and difficult. I learned the value and power of symbols — something which had been largely missing from my Christian education. I was being exposed to different ways of thinking and of seeing the world, and I was beginning to wonder if my way did justice to reality. What if things were not really as black and white as I'd been led to believe? My religious training had not taught me how to handle uncertainties, and I felt as if the earth was moving under my feet.

The last straw was when an intruder got into my digs and assaulted me. Although the assault was a minor one, I was devastated. The investigation by campus officials did not help. I had always been intensely shy and private, and now I was having to recount my experience to groups of rather forbidding men who seemed to me to be taking an unhealthy interest in the details. I was badly shaken by the whole experience; I felt unclean and deeply guilty.

I had always been taught, and firmly believed, that God was in control of every detail of my life. And hadn't he promised to solve all my problems? Why then was all this happening to me? I could no longer avoid facing the nagging question — *why was God doing this to me?* The negative feelings I had been repressing all my life would not be denied any longer, and I was overwhelmed.

I was shattered by the force of my anger and despair, and completely unable to deal with my feelings. I doubted that I was a Christian at all. But somehow, through those days of darkness I kept up my habit of daily Bible reading, and a surprising thing happened. I found that the feelings which I thought too shocking to voice were freely expressed within the sacred pages — and by some of God's holiest people! The psalmists, Elijah, Jeremiah, Job, Jonah, Martha, and Jesus himself all said the things

I dared not say. But if Jesus could cry 'My God, my God, why have you forsaken me', then surely so could I?

Still too uncertain to find my own words for my feelings, I began to use the words of Scripture to express them. Lamentations 3 was especially meaningful:

> I am the man who has seen affliction
>   by the rod of his [God's] wrath.
> He has driven me away and made me walk
>   in darkness rather than light;
> indeed, he has turned his hand against me
>   again and again, all day long.
>
> . . . He has beseiged me and surrounded me
>   with bitterness and hardship.
> He has made me dwell in darkness
>   like those long dead.
>
> He has walled me in so that I cannot escape;
>   he has weighed me down with chains.
> Even when I call out or cry for help,
>   he shuts out my prayer.
> He has barred my way with blocks of stone;
>   he has made my paths crooked.

Jeremiah describes God's brutal treatment of him for another seven verses before giving direct voice to his despair:

> I have been deprived of peace;
>   I have forgotten what prosperity is.
> So I say, 'My splendour is gone
>   and all that I had hoped from the Lord.'

> I remember my affliction and my wandering,
>   the bitterness and the gall.
> I well remember them,
>   and my soul is downcast within me.
> Yet this I call to mind
>   and therefore I have hope:
>
> Because of the Lord's great love we are not
>   consumed,
>   for his compassions never fail.
> They are new every morning;
>   great is your faithfulness.
> I say to myself, 'The Lord is my portion;
>   therefore I will wait for him.'
>
> . . . For men are not cast off
>   by the Lord for ever.
> Though he brings grief, he will show compassion,
>   so great is his unfailing love.
> For he does not willingly bring affliction
>   or grief to the children of men.
>   (Lam. 3:1–3, 7–9, 17–24, 31–33, *NIV*)

I read that passage often, and I used it to express my own bitterness, rage, and despair. I could not as yet feel the hope Jeremiah expressed towards the end of it, but I clung to the belief that I would get there some day.

And slowly I began to feel God's presence in a way I had never experienced before. I began to sense his interest and concern as I expressed my feelings to him. I began to rely on him for help, and found that he *did* help — not by altering the circumstances but by giving me courage and peace in facing them. I began to believe in God's love, not as an article of faith but as something

I was experiencing. It was the beginning of a new intimacy with God, a warmer relationship with him than I had ever thought possible.

I had stumbled on a vital principle: the importance of talking to God about what is *really* going on deep inside us. God values this inner truth and honesty; David's cry of penitence is, 'Surely you desire truth in the inner parts' (Ps. 51:6). An outward show of piety or a mental assent to doctrine are not enough; God is looking for an inner reality. He values that reality even when it is not 'nice'. Jesus clearly taught that what is in our hearts is much more important than our public face (Matt. 15:8–20, 23:25–28, cf. Luke 6:43–45). Honesty is essential even when our inner life seems unacceptable to us — and that is when we are most aware of our need of God. For that reason Jesus actually preferred the company of acknowledged sinners to that of the outwardly pious — something most of us still have difficulty coming to terms with. Our own priorities are very different!

The fact is that our thoughts and feelings are not always going to be sweet and pious, even when they concern God himself. Negative feelings are a part of all close relationships, and we have to learn to handle them if we want those relationships to develop into true intimacy. Our relationship with God is no exception. Sometimes it will fill us with joy, peace, and serenity; at other times it will be characterized on our part by anger, disappointment, confusion and resentment.

There can be many reasons for such feelings. Perhaps we feel God is making too many demands on us, encroaching too much on our territory. Dying to self is not a painless process, and anger often accompanies pain. For some people any kind of intimacy is painful, and love itself will provoke anger. Some, like Jeremiah, are called to tasks which involve them in hardship and rejection; it is inevitable that they will sometimes feel overwhelmed and resentful. For most of us there are times when, quite simply, God does not meet our expectations. This may be because his plans are different from ours, or because our expectations are false, or for no reason that we ever discover.

For those of us with charismatic leanings the problem can at times be especially acute. We believe that God can and does intervene supernaturally in people's lives. We have watched him do it a number of times, and read or heard of hundreds of miracles. *So why hasn't he intervened in my case?* The anguish of parents of terminally ill children is only heightened by hearing others' testimonies of healing. The disabled and dying are not helped to come to terms with their condition by continual encouragement to believe that they can be whole and well. Even worse is the implication that the fault lies with them. And healing isn't the only difficulty; in every area where we have faith to believe that God *could* intervene supernaturally, we have to come to terms with the fact that he sometimes chooses not to.

I recently had such an experience in the field of prophecy. Friends and colleagues had publicly been given wonderful prophetic words regarding their ministries and future. There was no such word for me, and the context was such that the omission seemed significant. It appeared that God had expressed his approval of them and not of me. Moreover, the lapse had been noted and commented on by others. Speculations about my future and my ministry grew. Some openly doubted that I had been called by God at all. In addition, I was facing a crossroads and needed to know what direction to take. I badly needed guidance and reassurance, and I prayed repeatedly that someone would have a word for me. After all, there were prophets around in plenty, and prophecies were multiplying. But God was silent. I too began to doubt that I was really called. I seriously considered leaving the ministry for secular work, and began to investigate openings.

At that point I attended a conference on renewal. One of the workshop leaders led us in a meditation on John 11, a passage I had myself written and preached on. John tells us that Lazarus was dying and Jesus, a close friend, was sent for. But Jesus refused to go and heal Lazarus. We were asked to imagine ourselves as Lazarus, growing weaker and weaker while waiting for the friend with the marvellous gift of healing — the friend who did not come. We imagined being on our deathbed, hope dying as each breath grew more laboured. We imagined lying in the darkness of the tomb. 'Why did you not come, Jesus? Why didn't you heal me?' Suddenly my own pain was released and I found myself screaming silently, 'Why wasn't there a prophecy for me? You could have spoken, God! *Why didn't you speak?*' I was shaken by my anger, but also relieved to have found expression for it. But still no word came.

Now, however, I found myself able to talk about my situation. And there were people to listen to me, people to tell me they believed God still wanted me in the ministry. Imperceptibly my courage was renewed. Over the next few weeks I was guided by ordinary means onto the right path. Within two months I had been called to a new sphere of ministry. Within five God had unmistakably renewed and reaffirmed his call to me and given me a new inner sense of vocation. He had not intervened supernaturally in the way I wanted, nor spared me the pain of misunderstanding and rejection. Nevertheless he had been in control of my future and working for my good.

Most of us have some experience of unanswered prayer. We have asked God for a job, a house, or a marriage partner — and gone without. God could have answered, but he has not. How have we handled it? Ultimately we have to accept his will, his way, and his timing, and our only peace is in doing so. But there is no shortcut to such acceptance; the route will take us through an honest expression of the hurt, confusion, and resentment that we feel. When it is all out in the open God has the chance to teach us something about his love, his ways and his purposes. But how often do we give ourselves or others the opportunity for such honest expression? Are our churches or home groups, or even our friendships, places where people can talk openly about their negative experiences and reactions as well as their positive ones? Such openness is a great stimulus to growth and fellowship.

All too often people who are struggling to come to terms with their growing disability, long-term unemployment, or continued singleness or childlessness have to do so on their own. There is usually some support available in a crisis, but we are not so good at facing the problems raised by ongoing difficulties. Perhaps we are too uncomfortable with those questions ourselves. Why is it that some people are healed while others remain disabled? Can Christ really give a sense of purpose to those for whom there is no job? Why is it that some conceive babies they do not want, while others bear only the heartache of childlessness? What does it *mean* to say that God loves such people? We don't treat our loved ones in such a way! Such questions become pressing for all of us at one time or another, but they lose much of their sting if they can be shared openly. Too often that is not the case.

Yet the Bible provides excellent precedents for doing so. The psalmists feel sometimes that God is unfair; Elijah believes God has let him down; Jeremiah thinks God has treated him cruelly and perversely. Nor are things necessarily any better for New Testament characters who come face to face with 'gentle Jesus meek and mild'.

Let's look at Lazarus' story from Martha's point of view. When she knew her brother Lazarus' life was in danger she and her sister Mary sent for Jesus to heal him. But Jesus did not come, and Lazarus died. Four days later Jesus finally arrived, apparently too late to help. Martha went to meet him and said, 'Lord, if you had been here, my brother would not have died.' Martha loved Jesus. She had faith in his power to heal, she called him Lord and believed he was the Son of God. She also believed that Jesus loved both her and her brother — and yet she expressed her anger that he had chosen not to come and heal Lazarus. Jesus had disappointed her, and that in a life and death matter. By any normal standards of friendship, she had a right to be angry; she had been badly let down.

And Jesus did not seem to be offended by her anger. The conversation that followed showed Martha to be the same strange mixture of belief and doubt, understanding and confusion, that most of us are. She was honest about those feelings and expressed them directly, not masking them with an artificial reverence. Far from being upset by that, Jesus respected it — and entrusted her with one of the most important statements about himself that he ever made:

> Jesus said to her [Martha], 'I am the resurrection and the life. He who believes in me will live, even though he dies; and whoever lives and believes in me will never die.' (John 11:25–26, *NIV*)

Of course the outcome was more glorious than Martha could ever have expected; Lazarus was raised from the dead. Jesus had delayed coming so a greater miracle could happen — but Martha couldn't have known that. In the meantime she had gone through agonies of grief and anger. She felt betrayed. The important thing was that she was honest enough to express those feelings to Jesus, so he could deal with them.

Of course it could be argued that the case is unusual. Our dead loved ones seldom come back to life in this world; there is not always an answer to our problems in the short term; and the reason for God's initial failure to act is not always so apparent. There are scars and burdens that we will have to bear for the rest of our lives, and we may never know the reason. This is not a perfect world — but one day God will make it so. Part of our pain is due to the fact that God sees things in the long term and we cannot. We do not see the glory that our sufferings are preparing for us.

In other (and less innocent) ways too our perspective is different from God's. This is illustrated by another occasion when Martha was angry with Jesus, but for rather a different reason. The occasion was a visit which Jesus and his disciples made to the home of Martha and Mary, and the story is told in Luke 10:38–42. Jesus had allowed Mary to sit in the living room with the men, when Martha needed her help in the kitchen. Martha was annoyed with Jesus for encouraging Mary's apparently selfish behaviour, and she let him know it. Jesus had again disappointed Martha's expectations and she resented it — but this time it was because he was operating from a different set of standards to her own. He thought it was more important that the women shared his company and his teaching than that they were perfect hostesses. The idea was a shocking one, completely overturning the customs of the day. Women were not permitted to receive religious instruction; their place was in the kitchen. No wonder that Martha was angry at Mary for taking the man's role, and at Jesus for letting her.

Jesus explained to Martha that his priorities were different from hers and those of society. We don't know whether Martha found the permission to learn as liberating as Mary did. We do know that when she encountered Jesus after Lazarus' death, she could express both her faith in him and her belief in the doctrine of the resurrection as clearly as any man. Would that have happened if she had remained fuming in the kitchen rather than getting the issue out in the open? Because Martha expressed her anger, Mary and all women were given explicit permission to learn, and that permission was recorded for all time. I for one am glad that she was angry!

Often we, like Martha, don't understand God's dealings with us because his standards, his methods, and his objectives are different from ours. It is natural that we feel confused, doubtful, and resentful. God understands that and wants to meet us in it, as he did Martha. We may find, as Job found, that we get no answers from God but that his presence is enough. It is when we encounter

God with our real selves that we can begin to understand his ways and his purposes. Gradually his standards become ours, and we find the peace and serenity we are looking for. But we will never attain it by pretending; only by letting God come close to us when we're least serene.

The wonder of it is that God accepts us exactly as we are, and is always ready to forgive us and to cleanse us from everything that is wrong. But he won't accept our pretence to be something we're not, our efforts to cover up the turmoil inside. He is saddened by our attempts to appear nicer and holier than we actually are. This is not because he is stern and unyielding in his demands for holiness, but because when we hide our hurt we prevent him from dealing with it.

I have a Bedlington terrier named Gandalf (Alfie for short). Occasionally Alfie gets a grass seed or a bit of sharp gravel wedged between his toes. He limps around woefully and makes fruitless attempts to remove the source of pain himself. It would be easy for me to do it, of course; but Alfie won't let me near the hurt paw. He's afraid of the extra pain involved in solving the problem. In the same way, we often try to hide our hurt from God rather than letting him deal with it. He wants us to trust him enough to let him get at the source of pain, to trust him not to hurt us more than is necessary. There is no other way to fully experience his love and his power to save.

2

The Shadow of the Almighty

He who dwells in the shelter of the Most High
will rest in the shadow of the Almighty.

(Ps. 91:1, NIV)

I swung higher and higher, right to the top of the arc our garden swingset would allow. As I swung with gusto I also sang with gusto, my favourite childhood hymn:

> When we walk with the Lord,
> In the light of his word
> What a glory he sheds on our way!
> While we do his good will
> He abides with us still,
> And with all who will trust and obey.
>
> Not a shadow can rise,
> Not a cloud in the skies,
> But his smile quickly drives it away;
> Not a doubt nor a fear,
> Not a sigh nor a tear
> Can abide while we trust and obey.[1]

I loved that hymn; its confidence and simplicity were so comforting. I loved its promise that 'Not a cloud . . . can abide while we trust and obey'. But another favourite, a religious poem, carried a different message:

God hath not promised
Skies always blue
Flower-strewn pathways
All the way through. . .[2]

Those two bits of verse now seem symbolic of two different attitudes to spirituality: God means you never have to say you're hurting; and God knows it won't always be easy! For most of my life I have been swinging like a pendulum between these two attitudes. The tension springs partly from my emotional make-up, which swings easily from high to low. I think it also has something to do with the contrast between the two main spiritual influences on my childhood — the Church and my father. The Church was represented not only by our local church but also by the many conference centres we visited each summer as part of my father's job. They preached (and sang) a simple Christianity, a victorious Christianity. Jesus had already won the victory; because we belonged to him we could and should be 'living in the victory' too. This is quite right up to a point; we should be experiencing a victory over sin and temptation. But the implication was that we should also be 'victorious' over suffering and the trials of life — that they should never get us down. The 'abundant life' was the key phrase; a radiant and joyful life, a life of better quality than any non-Christian could hope to have.

The picture presented was often an idealized one. Prayer was pure bliss:

I walk in the garden alone
While the dew is still on the roses. . .
And he walks with me, and he talks with me

> And he tells me I am his own;
> And the joy we share as we tarry there
> No other can ever know.[3]

And nothing disturbed the believer's fellowship with God:

> Every day with Jesus is sweeter than the day before;
> Every day with Jesus I love him more and more. . .[4]

None of this was automatic, of course; for

> . . . we never can prove
> The delights of his love
> Until all on the altar we lay,
> For the favour he shows
> And the joy he bestows
> Are for them who will trust and obey.[5]

I was sure that if I were really committed, if I really loved God, then my feelings towards him would always be warm and glowing. He, in turn, would answer my prayers, solve my difficulties, and smoothe my path through life. These expectations were largely subconscious; if someone had stated them to me so baldly I would probably have denied it. Nevertheless they were real.

But that was only one side of the story. My father brought to bear a very different influence. He was more in tune with 'God hath not promised skies always blue'. He too had a firm evangelical faith, and in fact was much in demand as a preacher. But his own spiritual heritage was that of the Puritans rather than twentieth-century revivalists. He was an intellectual who had been much

influenced by Martyn Lloyd-Jones, and was at home with
the questioning attitudes of university students. He had
a sense of humour and was impatient with the cosy, senti-
mental view of the Christian life. On one occasion my
Sunday School teacher told us that we ought never to go
to the cinema because 'can you imagine Jesus going to
the cinema?' My father's response was robust: 'No, but
I can't imagine him going to the toilet either, and I'm
sure he did!' On another occasion he prepared himself to
lead Sunday worship while singing:

> When upon life's billows you are tempest tossed
> Take a seasick pill before your all is lost!

His Puritan theology did not lend itself to optimism,
emphasizing as it did the sinfulness and guilt of human
beings, and the strict demands made on us by God. It
was essentially a stern view of life. His own life had
been hard, and his ministry often involved him and us in
sacrifice and conflict. I was fiercely loyal to my parents
and adored my father in particular, with his commanding
personality, his spiritual confidence and his successful
ministry. I knew my parents were devoted to God and in
my eyes they could do no wrong; yet I could not help but
be aware that life was often a real struggle for them. They
trusted and obeyed, but their (and our) lives were often
clouded by hardship and anxiety. Their attitude to God
and the Christian life reflected that.

The different spiritualities I encountered within and
outside our home might well have given me a pretty
balanced outlook — but I could not integrate them.
Instead, I repeatedly swung between one and the other.
Part of me was attracted to expectant, optimistic and

vibrant Christianity; another part of me was more serious, expecting only trouble! When at the age of 17 I encountered the then new charismatic movement it appealed instantly to the first side of me, and I embraced it wholeheartedly. The experience of the Spirit I had then was genuine and life-changing, and more than 20 years on I still regard it as one of the most significant events of my life. But charismatic theology could not help me cope with adversity, and I found charismatic worship impossible in the hard times.

So I continued to swing, every few years, between the Reformed and the charismatic. When with charismatics I missed the thoughtfulness, depth, and stability of Reformed churches; when in Reformed churches I missed the life, spontaneity, and confidence in God that the charismatics had. The one could not help me with the hard experiences of life, nor cope with the questions I was always asking. The other lacked so much of what I knew to be real and valid in Christian experience. Eventually I discovered that within the Church of England it was possible to be both charismatic and Reformed. I also found things which were new to me: tradition, liturgy, the church year, religious symbols. I began to explore these, while at the same time maintaining and extending my charismatic experience and theology. In due course I was ordained and began to work full-time in the Church.

Then something very strange happened. I had been used to getting clear impressions of what God wanted to say, either in words or in mental pictures – often both. This happened in prayer meetings, counselling sessions, church services, and when praying on my own. When I passed on what I thought God was giving to me, people generally responded positively. When I prepared sermons

I had a clear conviction of what God wanted to say from the Bible passage we were looking at. Life wasn't always easy, and ministry was often a struggle. Nevertheless, I had a strong sense of God's immediacy, of his concern. Almost daily I experienced signs of his presence; it was exciting and encouraging.

Then suddenly, almost overnight, all of this stopped. I no longer felt God's presence with me. There were no pictures, no prophecies, no words from God. When I preached I did not have the same sense of authority, the same conviction that *this* was God's word for the people — though the response was much as it had been before. When I prayed God seemed to have left the room. Praying in tongues became impossible, and my mind simply would not form the words to pray in English. When I read the Bible, which had always been the focus of my life, I could make no sense of the words in front of me. I felt as if I had been turned upside down and lost my bearings. My security and my certainty had gone from me. At the end of one particularly confusing day I lay in the bath and said, 'God, I'm not certain any more who I am or what I believe. But I know that I love you and that you love me . . . and for now that's enough.'

And, oddly, it *was* enough. Gone were the signs of God's presence in my life that I had come to depend on. I could no longer experience his presence in the emotional, intuitive and intellectual ways that I was used to. Yet in some other way, perhaps with some other faculty, I began to sense that he was there, and even (ridiculously) that he was in what was happening to me. I spent hours 'thinking' about him, but without seeming to use my mind. In those times of silence I felt his presence, but my emotions were bypassed completely. I could not make head nor tail of it. It was as if he were speaking to me by means of his very absence. It was especially confusing because for the previous two years I had been influenced by the teaching that God's presence is indicated by signs and wonders. Now all the signs had gone, and the only wonder was that I still believed God loved me!

I remembered that St Teresa and St John of the Cross had taught about an experience of this kind, calling it the 'dark night of the soul'. They described the 'dark night' as a phase when God seems remote, the signs of his presence in our lives disappear, and prayer becomes impossible. But it is actually a stage in growth, a time of maturing. I knew little more about it than that, but it sounded promising. I wanted to know more, and I knew where to go for help. Sister Hilda was an Anglican nun whom I had seen from time to time as part of the diocese's 'senior friend' scheme. From a Strict Methodist background herself, she understood my evangelicalism; yet she was trained in classical spirituality and spiritual direction. She had also the assets of a medical training, a theology degree, a lively mind, and a keen sense of humour. She needed that — I managed to knock her wimple off at our first meeting! For over a year we met regularly to talk about how God deals with us spiritually, emotionally and psychologically. We started by studying together St Teresa's book *The Interior Castle*.

St Teresa wrote of experiences which sounded remarkably like charismatic phenomena: words of knowledge, being slain in the spirit, and visionary trances. These 'spiritual consolations' are valuable — but not to be sought out. They are only a stage on the way to spiritual maturity:

> There are souls who start, advance half way and experi-
> ence . . . the sweet comforts God gives. Then they
> think they should enjoy these pleasures continually.
> I've said it before: they should stop giving themselves
> up to this absorption so much.[6]

Instead, they should meditate on the suffering of Jesus.

According to both St Teresa and St John of the Cross, these enjoyable spiritual experiences are liable to disappear and leave the believer feeling confused and desolate. The Christian is being drawn away from the signs of God's presence, which can be distractions, to seek God for himself. Our love for God is tested when we get no emotional satisfaction from him.

> Often it is to the weakest that His Divine Majesty gives
> favours, and I suppose they would not exchange these
> for the strength of Christians who serve God in arid-
> ness. We love spiritual consolations more than the
> Cross! Test us, O Lord, you who know all truth, so
> that we may know ourselves.[7]

At last! Someone who believed charismatic experience to be genuine and valuable, but also believed that there was more. All of this rang true and was very helpful; it encouraged me to carry on.

At about the same time I reread Charles Spurgeon's *Lectures to his Students*. Spurgeon, the great Victorian Baptist preacher, was a Spirit-led man who sometimes exercised in his ministry what we would call words of knowledge. He also founded and ran a training college for young Baptist ministers. The lectures he gave them are still in print today, and their faith, wit, and common sense are as striking as ever. One chapter in particular interested me. It's called 'The Minister's Fainting Fits'.

The lesson of wisdom is, *Be not dismayed by soul-trouble*. Count it no strange thing, but a part of ordinary spiritual experience. . . Put no trust in frames and feelings. Care more for a grain of faith than a ton of excitement. . . Serve God with all your might while the candle is burning, and then when it goes out for a season, you will have less to regret. . . Any simpleton can follow the narrow path in the light: faith's rare wisdom enables us to march on in the dark with infallible accuracy . . . be it ours, when we cannot see the face of our God, to trust under the shadow of his wings.[8]

All this tallied remarkably well not only with what I was then experiencing, but also with a prophecy we had recently received at the church where I then was: 'Seek my face, not my hands.' We were to want God for who he is, not for what he could give us. There had also been a prophecy that some people would find the ways in which they normally experienced God beginning to change. It all seemed to be adding up. What was happening to me was a normal part of spiritual experience, though one that I had heard little about in all my years in churches. It seemed to fit in with the experience of great saints of the past, and with up-to-the-minute prophecy. So far so good. But could it be found in the teaching of the Bible?

I knew that the Bible did describe times of difficulty and darkness for those who follow God. Now I went back for another look at what it had to say. It was obvious that the prophets had not found following God easy.

Elijah's despair under the broom tree, or Jeremiah's bitterness in Lamentations, are two obvious examples. We
can only guess at Hosea's grief as his warnings were
rejected again and again, and he had to watch doom
approaching himself and his country. He must have suffered more than any of his compatriots: he was aware of
the full extent of the disaster, and the possibility of avoiding it, as no one else was. And did he never question why
God had added to his personal grief by directing him to
marry a prostitute? I can just picture Hosea touring the
brothels, looking for his missing wife and singing, 'Not a
sigh nor a tear can abide while we trust and obey'!

God looks after his people with the tender care of a
mother for her newborn infant . . . but he also asked
Abraham to sacrifice his only son. He is the God whose
voice 'shatters cedars':

> Yahweh's voice carves out lightning-shafts,
> Yahweh's voice convulses the desert,
> Yahweh's voice . . . strips forests bare.
>
> (Ps. 29:5, 7–9)

Again and again we read that God is surrounded by
darkness and cloud. 'Cloud, black cloud enfolds him' (Ps.
97:2); he has 'a storm-cloud underneath his feet' and
'wrapped himself in darkness' (2 Sam. 22:10, 12);
'Yahweh has chosen to dwell in thick cloud' (1 Kings
8:12; 2 Chron. 6:1).

If God lives in thick darkness, no wonder that those
close to him are sometimes in darkness too! Perhaps it
shields us from being burnt up by the blazing splendour
of his presence when we become close to him. Nevertheless, it can be difficult to endure. How are we to cope?

'Which of you walks in darkness and sees no light? Let him trust in the name of Yahweh and lean on his God!' (Isa. 50:10). The only way through is to keep trusting, to keep walking in faith though all the good feelings are gone – just as we do when they are readily on tap. As C. S. Lewis once said, there is no sight that frightens the devil more than that of a believer for whom all trace of God has disappeared from the world, who nevertheless gets on his or her knees to pray.

We can see this in Jesus' own ministry. He performed many signs and miracles. He made sick people well, set free the demonized, walked on water, changed water into wine. It must have been tremendously exciting. But Jesus also told his disciples not to look for miracles: 'a wicked and adulterous generation asks for a miraculous sign' (Matt. 12:39, 16:4; Mark 8:12; Luke 11:16, 29). He encouraged obedience rather than religious sentiment (Luke 11:27–28).

I had long understood Jesus' post-resurrection appearances in a similar light. Jesus' identity was generally 'hidden' from his disciples; 'they were kept from recognizing him'. They were weaned away from dependence on the physical signs of his presence; what Jesus looked and sounded like, his touch, his smile, his voice. This was to prepare them to recognize his presence by faith, in their spirits. They were to know the presence of Jesus by the resemblance of someone's teaching to his, or by the works that were done by Jesus through someone with a different physical presence, but with the same Holy Spirit. If our faith is to be developed we have constantly to recognize the same Jesus coming to us in different ways, through different people. Often we have to experience the loss of the spiritual comforts that we are used to in order to receive new blessings. While our hands are full of old treasures we cannot pick up new ones; we have first to let go of what we are holding on to.

All this made a lot of sense. But why should the spiritual life involve darkness and pain, when Jesus had come to redeem us from all that? Jesus did not say he came to make us happy or carefree — he came to make us whole. He came to help us to live life in all its fullness. To live life to the full is to allow ourselves fully to experience all that life offers us — the joys, the sorrows, the uncertainties, the risks, the satisfactions. The extent to which we cut ourselves off from any of these is the extent to which we turn our backs on life. The ability to experience the bad as well as the good is the measure of a complete human being, and essential for psychological health. The psychiatrist M. Scott Peck writes:

> . . . it is often the most spiritually healthy and advanced among us who are called to suffer in ways more agonizing than anything experienced by the more ordinary. Great leaders, when wise and well, are likely to endure degrees of anguish unknown to the common man. Conversely, it is the unwillingness to suffer emotional pain that usually lies at the very root of emotional illness. Those who fully experience depression, doubt, confusion, and despair may be infinitely more healthy than those who are generally certain, complacent, and self-satisfied.[9]

If we let the Spirit of God have full play in our personalities he will develop our capacities. As our spiritual perception increases we will become more sensitive to bad as well as good. As we see the potential in people or situations with his eyes, so we experience his grief when that potential is not realized. We feel God's pain and anger when we encounter injustice, cruelty, manipulation or deception. To open ourselves up to God is to experience 'bad' feelings as well as 'good' ones. That, after all, is what it means for him to open himself up to the world. We cannot share his life, his heart, without also sharing his pain.

Although my own 'dark night' seemed to be a time of emptiness and confusion, in retrospect I know that I was greatly enriched by it. My core beliefs are the same as they were before – but the *way* I believe is very different. I am less certain but more sure. That is, I am less certain of a particular system of belief, but much more sure of God and his love. And with that sureness has come an inner rest. My prayer life, too, is different. I spend less time in intercession, more time in contemplation. Often I just sit and let God's presence fill me. There is no need for words. Even when I pray for others I often carry them into God's presence and hold them there, without making any particular request. It seems at least as effective as the anxious pleading and claiming I used to do. I am more relaxed with God, more relaxed with myself, more relaxed with people who hold different views than my own. I am glad now that I let the darkness come upon me.

'Yahweh has chosen to dwell in a thick cloud.' Let us then be willing to live sometimes in cloud and confusion. And when the darkness comes let us try to be still, and rest in the shadow of the Almighty.

3

Glory!

With mercy and with judgment
  My web of time he wove,
And aye the dews of sorrow
  Were lustred by his love;
I'll bless the hand that guided,
  I'll bless the heart that planned,
When throned where glory dwelleth
  In Immanuel's land.[1]

I believe in the Kingdom Come
Then all the colours will bleed into one
But yes I'm still running
You broke the bonds
You loosed the chains
You carried the cross
And my shame
And my shame
You know I believe it
But I still haven't found
What I'm looking for
But I still haven't found
What I'm looking for[2]

I put my new cassette into the tape recorder. Dionne
Warwick's limpid tones floated through the house:
'What's it all about, Alfie? Is it just for the moment we

live?' My dog Alfie trotted obediently in from the next room and nuzzled the tape recorder. He obeyed the summons but couldn't answer the question. Neither can most of us . . . but it's one of the most important questions we can ever ask. What *is* life all about? Is there more to it than the present moment, more to live for? It is probable that most Christians will immediately answer 'yes!' And for evangelicals, it is taken as read that being a Christian will give us a new sense of purpose, that our lives take on new meaning when we are converted. But I wonder how many of us could answer with clarity if the question were pressed further: *exactly* what is the purpose in life of a Christian? Is it to save souls, as I've sometimes been told? Then what happens if we are not very good at it? How many people have to be converted before we have achieved our purpose in life — a hundred? fifty? ten? Will our life still have meaning if we only ever lead one person to the Lord? What if we witness and witness and witness and no one ever responds? What of children who die too young to have done any evangelizing, or the disabled who are unable to get out and meet people? Have their lives had no purpose?

The catechism describes the purpose of our lives in rather different terms: 'the chief end of man [and woman!] is to glorify God and enjoy him for ever'. I like the sound of enjoying God — that sounds almost too good to be true. But what exactly does it mean to glorify him? The Bible tells us of at least five ways in which we can glorify God.

The first and most obvious way is *by praising him*. There has been a good deal of excellent teaching about this in recent years, and we will be looking at praise in the next chapter. But I will note here that one mark of

God's hand on someone's life is their readiness to praise God. As praise in the Bible principally means telling what God is like and what he has done, this involves a thoughtful awareness of what God is doing in us and in the world. It is not simply a mindless response, or a handy way of punctuating conversations.

Second, *we glorify God when we are like him in character*. Jesus said, 'It is to the glory of my Father that you should bear much fruit and be my disciples' (John 15:8). And what is fruit? Is it conversions? No, 'the fruit of the Spirit is love, joy, peace, patience, kindness, goodness, faithfulness [lit. 'good faith', 'honesty', 'integrity'], gentleness and self-control' (Gal. 5:22, *NIV*). That describes God's personality, although it is not a complete description. The Bible tells us many other things about God's nature too. For instance, God is wisdom (Prov. 3:19; Isa. 11:2; Eph. 1:17); and so is Jesus (Luke 2:40; Matt. 13:54; 1 Cor. 1:24, 30). God is truth (Ps. 31:5; Isa. 45:19, 65:16; John 14:17, 15:26; Col. 1:6; 1 John 5:6); and so is Jesus (John 1:14, 14:6). Notice that I said not 'God is wise and truthful' but 'God is wisdom and truth'. Similarly, God is not just loving; he *is* love (1 Cor. 13; 1 John 4:8). Wisdom, truth, and love are so utterly of his essence that he *is* them. John said of Jesus, 'we saw his glory, the glory that he has from the Father as only Son of the Father, full of grace and truth' (John 1:14).

We were made in God's image, to be like him. Although God's image in us was tarnished by the Fall, we now have God's Spirit to produce God's character in us. And when the characteristics of God's personality shine through the personality which is unique to us, God is glorified. As Paul says:

All of us, with our unveiled faces like mirrors reflecting the glory of the Lord, are being transformed into the image that we reflect in brighter and brighter glory; this is the working of the Lord who is the Spirit. (2 Cor. 3:18)

Third, *we glorify God when we are like him not only in our character but also in our deeds;* and what we do is the result of who we are. Jesus urged his disciples, 'Your light must shine in people's sight, so that, seeing your good works, they may give praise to your Father in heaven' (Matt. 5:16). And Paul concludes a passage on the wonder of being saved by grace, with this marvellous statement: 'We are God's work of art, created in Christ Jesus for the good works which God has already designated to make up our way of life' (Eph. 2:10). God has made each of us the way we are so that we can do certain good works — and they will be different for each of us. In theory this should fill us with excitement at discovering our own mission in life, and relieve us of the guilt of not doing everything. In practice, many of us face so many demands on our prayers, our giving, our time, and our concern that we constantly feel guilty and inadequate. We are limited human beings. None of us can be wrung with pity for the starving of Africa, the orphans of Eastern Europe, the refugees of Asia, the homeless and the unemployed of our own country, and the private crises of our friends and neighbours . . . all at the same time.

Nor does God ask it. He asks that we do the specific good works which he has designed us individually to do. With each issue that comes to our attention it is worth asking, 'Do you want me to do something about this? If so, what?' God may want us to invest five minutes of prayer, or £10, or a lifetime's commitment. 'Our' good works may be counselling, healing people, sitting on church committees, secular voluntary work, hospitality, doing an elderly neighbour's garden . . . the list is endless. Whatever it is that we are cut out to do, in the doing of it we will find satisfaction ourselves and bring glory to God. Often we feel obliged to get involved in something we were not really designed for, and it proves draining and frustrating. Sometimes, indeed, the only way to find out is by trial and error. But there is no point in carrying a load of guilt because we think what we are doing is unimportant, or because we are aware of needs we cannot meet. If meeting a particular need is not our job it will be someone else's; we must leave it to God to draw that person's attention to it.

Paul prayed for the Colossians that:

> . . . through perfect wisdom and spiritual understanding you should reach the fullest knowledge of his will and so be able to lead a life worthy of the Lord, a life acceptable to him in all its aspects, bearing fruit in every kind of good work and growing in knowledge of God, fortified, in accordance with his glorious strength, with all power always to persevere and endure, giving thanks with joy to the Father who has made you able to share the lot of God's holy people and with them to inherit the light. (Col. 1:9b–12)

'Good works' are not necessary for our salvation, but they are an essential part of God's plan for each one of us. The doing of them will require wisdom and spiritual understanding, endurance, and the power of a mighty God working within us; in fact, all of God's resources for us. The result will be joyous; help for others, fulfilment for ourselves, and glory for God.

Fourth, *we glorify God when we help other people to become Christians*. Jesus taught that there is rejoicing in heaven when a sinner repents (Luke 15:7). There is rejoicing on earth too; Paul says that 'as grace spreads, so, to the glory of God, thanksgiving may also overflow among more and more people' (2 Cor. 4:15). Every time someone turns to God and is brought from darkness to light, it glorifies God in heaven and on earth, for it shows his power and his love. We will be looking at honesty in our witness in a later chapter, so let us turn to our final point.

Fifth, *we glorify God in our suffering*. What an outrageous idea! How can human suffering possibly bring glory to God? Yet the Bible clearly says that it can and does. John says that Jesus 'indicated the kind of death by which Peter would give glory to God' (John 21:19). Throughout the New Testament suffering is linked with glory . . . both our glory and God's glory. This is the way of glory which we least understand and most often overlook, so it is worth spending some time on it here.

Let's start with the example of a Christian family with two adorable young children, Angela and Andrew, who both suffer from a rare genetic disorder which means they are frequently very ill and in pain. They need complicated medical care and occasional surgery. Their church has prayed frequently and fervently for their healing, and hands have been laid on them by people famous for their healing ministry. Sometimes a temporary improvement has occurred, but the underlying condition has not been healed. What had these youngsters ever done to deserve disability and pain? What had their parents done to deserve such anguish and anxiety? Why hasn't God healed them? I wrestled with these questions. Eventually I took them to Sister Hilda, who worked in the children's hospice where they sometimes went for treatment.

'Yes, it's very difficult,' she said, 'but Angela and Andrew are fulfilling their purpose in life. They are glorifying God.'

'How?', I asked. 'How can the suffering of innocent children ever bring glory to a God who is supposed to be loving?'

Sister Hilda replied, 'I wish you could have seen them here last week. There they were, despite their pain, teaching the other children and parents a song about the love of God. And joy was written all over their faces. They were glorifying God.'

It's not suffering in itself which glorifies God, but the way in which we handle suffering. If we are not defeated by suffering, if it is obvious that God is giving us strength and joy despite everything, then he is glorified. He is demonstrating what is possible for a human being who has the resources of God at his or her disposal. I still have a picture which I cut out of a magazine when I was about ten years old. It shows a beautiful wildflower growing out of a solid rock face. The caption reads, 'The pursuit of excellence in the face of adversity is invariably matched by the glory of the result.' The Christian life, for many, might well be described as 'the pursuit of excellence in the face of adversity'. The result will certainly be glory, though we might doubt that we've achieved excellence. It is continuing to pursue it that matters, continuing to reach out for God's best.

Again and again God takes his chosen ones to the end

of their strength, their faith, their endurance. As Paul wrote:

> We hold this treasure in pots of earthenware, so that the immensity of the power is God's and not our own. We are subjected to every kind of hardship, but never distressed; we see no way out but we never despair; we are pursued but never cut off; knocked down, but still have some life in us; always we carry with us in our body the death of Jesus so that the life of Jesus, too, may be visible in our body. (2 Cor. 4:7–10)

We are pushed to the edge of our limitations so that we may transcend them; to the edge of our humanity so that we may live the life of the divine. It is not an easy process.

The message of the New Testament is quite clear: the way to life is through death; the way to joy is through pain. Jesus said, 'If anyone wants to be a follower of mine, let him renounce himself and take up his cross and follow me. Anyone who wants to save his life will lose it; but anyone who loses his life for my sake will find it' (Matt. 16:24–25; cf. Matt. 10:38–39; Mark 8:34; Luke 9:23, 14:27). Other New Testament writers develop the theme, for example:

> We must all experience many hardships before we enter the kingdom of God. (Acts 14:22)

> The temporary, light burden of our hardships is earning us for ever an utterly incomparable, eternal weight of glory, since what we aim for is not visible but invisible. (2 Cor. 4:17)

Let us exult, too, in our hardships, understanding that

hardship develops perseverance, and perseverance
develops a tested character, something that gives us
hope, and a hope which will not let us down, because
the love of God has been poured into our hearts by
the Holy Spirit which has been given to us. (Rom.
5:3–5; cf. Jas. 1:2–4)

Hope is a direct result, not of ease, as you might expect,
but of hardship. It comes from finding that however low
we get, God's arms are still beneath us; however desper-
ate our situation, he has resources to meet it. There is
no situation that defeats him, no evil from which he
cannot produce something good. He turns our darkness
into light; he makes all things beautiful in their time. *In
their time* — that's the problem. We want a solution, an
answer, *now*!

Some time ago I attended the funeral of a middle-aged
woman who had never married or had children. Janet
Marshall came from a small family, lived on her own and
held down a routine clerical job. Yet several hundred
turned out on a weekday to attend her funeral, and their
grief and sense of loss were deeply felt. What had this
woman achieved that was so special? Simply this; she had
been born a paraplegic, and living a normal life had been
pronounced impossible by her doctors. But Janet was not
easily conquered by adversity. After one long spell of
illness she was made redundant by the firm for whom she
had worked for 15 years. But Janet did not give up.
Instead, she retrained as a VDU operator and got another
job. And although living alone and working for a living
are challenge enough for someone with little use of their
limbs, Janet was not content to leave it at that. She was
a committed church member and attended Bible studies

regularly; she was a Girl Guide leader, she invited people to dinner in her flat, and she organized theatre parties. She had one of the most unquenchable spirits I have ever encountered. When I was with her I felt I had gained from her vitality — and that was the experience of all who knew her.

Janet was never healed of her disability. There was never a chance for newspaper or magazine headlines to proclaim God's amazing power to heal, no book telling her miracle story. But there was a miracle, no question about it. And no seven-day wonder, either, but fifty-odd years of remarkable testimony to the grace and love of God in difficult circumstances, and to the strength he can give a human spirit. Janet was not healed, to the glory of God.

Janet's disability gave her reason enough to withdraw into herself; surviving was hard work, and she was different from those around her. But instead of withdrawing Janet reached out to others. She had a gift for encouragement, for drawing people out of themselves. Hardship often makes people bitter, and suffering may lead us to question the love of God. When we radiate the love of God *despite* our suffering, then God is glorified. In Romans 5 Paul links suffering with hardship, hardship with hope, and all of them with the pouring of the love of God into our hearts. But this does not happen automatically. It happens when we invite God into our suffering.

Growth in the Christian life is a process of exchanging our faulty nature for God's perfect one; the process is accelerated at times when we are more than usually aware of our need. But if our expectation is that God will always make things easy for us, then in our resentment at being 'let down' we may not let him get close enough to us to pour his love into our hearts. Alternatively we may be so bent on proving how brave, forgiving, or spiritual we are in a crisis, that we refuse to admit to our distress. This, too, prevents God from meeting us in our pain. Both attitudes will short-circuit the process of growth and transformation which God in his compassion intends for us.

Janet's handicap was physical; ours may be emotional or psychological. We may be incapable of rising above smaller difficulties than those she triumphed over so superbly. That is nothing to be ashamed of; it is the way God made us. It helps if we can learn to see our emotional and psychological shortcomings as a kind of disability in which God can show the glory of his love. Of course this is immensely difficult, because such things seem to be so much a part of the essential 'us'. They may by their very nature prevent us from seeing what is good in ourselves or in our situation, and produce a feeling of distance from God which is very far from being the truth. How can God's love and glory be demonstrated then?

John Newton and William Cowper were close friends who lived in the same small village in Buckinghamshire. Both were outstanding witnesses in the eighteenth century, and since, to the power of God's love in a human personality. John Newton captained a slave ship, was dramatically converted, and eventually became a noted preacher and campaigner against slavery. A remarkable example of how God can change the personality of a cruel and depraved man, he wrote the famous hymn:

> Amazing grace! how sweet the sound
> That saved a wretch like me:

I once was lost, but now am found;
Was blind, but now I see.

William Cowper, son of a chaplain to the king, was a
gentle poet who was subject all his life to severe suicidal
depressions. So crippling were they that he was unable
to live alone, and for much of his life had to live under
the guardianship of others. Yet through it all he hung on
somehow to his faith in God, a God who is seen at work
in sorrow:

God moves in a mysterious way
His wonders to perform;
He plants his footsteps in the sea,
And rides upon the storm.

Ye fearful saints, fresh courage take,
The clouds ye so much dread
Are big with mercy, and shall break
In blessings on your head.

Cowper named that poem 'Light Shining Out of Darkness', and it might well have served as a motto for his own
life. Out of his vulnerability to uncertainty and despair
he wrote hymns which have strengthened many: 'Jesus,
where'er thy people meet/There they behold thy mercy-
seat' and 'Oh! for a closer walk with God'. Together
Newton and Cowper wrote a hymnbook which was used
in the renewal movement of their day; some of those
hymns are still loved and sung now. They were very
different people, but they both showed in their lives the
glory of God.

That's easy to see, of course, from the perspective of

more than two centuries. I doubt whether Cowper, in the midst of his depression, had any notion that he was glorifying God. Or whether he felt grateful, when recovering from one of his suicide attempts, for the love of a God who would not let him die when he so desperately wanted to. Similarly we may be quite unable to see any kind of purpose in our troubles, simply because we are too close to them. But if we look at the way God has been glorified in the sufferings of others, we can be confident that he can be glorified in our sufferings too. It is just that we may be the last to know!

In the meantime we want an answer . . . *now*. We are unlikely to get it. Instead, we are pressed to the limits of our endurance, only to find that we can endure some more. With God's Spirit within us, we are stronger people than we were. We are never completely defeated. Even if we suffer depression, mental illness, or a nervous breakdown God is there with us. We learn about his acceptance, his grace, his compassion for us in our weakness — and his love for other people who suffer similarly. We can pass on to others the comfort God has given us in our extremity.

Of course suffering is not the whole story: Jesus' own contemporaries were shocked at his ability to enjoy himself. Sinners found him good company; it was the religious people who were uncomfortable with him. There was nothing of the prude or the killjoy about him. He had, after all, come to bring abundant life. But what *is* abundant life? Quite simply, it is life in all its abundance, with all its variety and richness. Jesus came that we might have life in all its potential — both in this world and in the next. In this world life consists of very mixed experiences for good and bad alike: he 'sends down rain to fall on the upright and the wicked alike' (Matt. 5:45). If anything, life can be harder for God's people: 'If our hope in Christ has been for this life only, we are of all people the most pitiable' (1 Cor. 15:19). Yet because we know that this is God's world and is to be enjoyed, we live our lives here with zest. We can take risks, because we have less to lose than most people. After all, we know that God loves us and can make the best of any mistakes that we make; and we look forward to another life in a better world.

We can learn to accept both pleasure and pain from God's hand; ease and hardship for our spirits as well as our bodies. Unfortunately, many of us assume that once we are adopted into God's family and filled with his Spirit, all spiritual experiences will be pleasant and even exciting. For several years I took as my motto the verse 'I want to know Christ and the power of his resurrection' (Phil. 3:10, *NIV*). It was with some shock that I eventually realized the verse continues, 'and the fellowship of sharing in his sufferings, becoming like him in his death. . .' There was not even a comma between the two phrases, but I had somehow missed the second half of the verse. I suspect it was because it seemed so much less attractive!

In fact the early Christians counted it a very great privilege to share in the sufferings of Christ. God is lavish with his blessings, and many experience God's power in healings and miracles who have no wish to become close to him. The Gospels record that Jesus healed many who never so much as came back to say thank you; one man even reported him to the authorities. Of the five thousand who ate the bread and fish which Jesus had miraculously multiplied, how many followed him closely? Only a few, and those few were called to share the hardships which he endured. When the mother of James and John asked for special places in God's kingdom for her sons, Jesus' reply was that such places would be theirs if they could share his cup of suffering. The terms have not changed. We cannot be a member of a human family without sharing that family's trials and tribulations; we cannot be a member of God's family without sharing his suffering.

It is easy to see how Jesus' disciples shared his suffering; they were beaten, imprisoned, exiled, and executed for being Christians. But surely our pain, of whatever sort, has nothing to do with the suffering of Christ? I think that it has. God's suffering for the world was focused on the cross, but it is not limited to that time and that event. The Scriptures make it plain that God yearns continually over the people he has made. He grieves at our hardheartedness, our rejection of him, our cruelty to each other. And in that remarkable passage in Romans 8:18–27, Paul has the created world, the people of God, and the Holy Spirit all groaning together in frustration at the futility of the world as it now is.

Our mental and emotional pain in a broken world may well be a sharing in the suffering of Christ. When we are grieved by the waste of so many lives that never reach their potential; when we are angered at the heartlessness of politicians, generals, and bureaucrats; when we are sickened by the violence we see on the news; when we are brought low by the meaninglessness of it all; then we are sharing in the suffering of Christ. And the willingness to be sensitive to such things carries with it an increased sensitivity to our own pain, so that too becomes part of the burden we carry for Christ. Thus even our depressions may be redemptive, for others as well as for ourselves. Paul spoke of completing 'what is still lacking in regard to Christ's afflictions, for the sake of his body, which is the church' (Col. 1:24, *NIV*). It is a mystery to me why this should be or how it works, but it may go some way towards explaining why things so often go wrong for Christians, and why so many people who are close to God are subject to depression.

That sense of futility which is so dark a part of depression is sometimes the product of a true vision of God, and the potential he has given ourselves and our world — a potential which is largely wasted in this life. So Browning understood when he put a monologue into the mouth of Andrea del Sarto, an Italian painter known for his perfect technique. Del Sarto has sacrificed his artistic integrity in order to make money; he has stopped striving and stretching himself. The other painters achieve:

> so much less!
> Well, less is more, Lucrezia: I am judged.
> There burns a truer light of God in them,
> In their vexed beating stuffed and stopped-up brain,
> Heart, or whate'er else, than goes on to prompt
> This low-pulsed forthright craftsman's hand of mine.
> Their works drop groundward, but themselves, I
>   know,
> Reach many a time a heaven that's shut to me,
> Enter and take their place there sure enough,
> Though they come back and cannot tell the world.
> My works are nearer heaven, but I sit here. . .
> Ah! But a man's reach should exceed his grasp,
> Or what's a heaven for?[3]

Dissatisfaction with the world as it is may well result from seeing things from God's perspective. Nevertheless we are not gloomy people, for we have hope. Our divine dissatisfaction points to a better world. That's what heaven's for.

The Bible clearly links suffering in this life with glory, both in this life and in the next. Paul tells us that we are:

> . . . heirs of God and joint-heirs with Christ, provided that we share his suffering, so as to share his glory. In my estimation, all that we suffer in the present time is nothing in comparison with the glory which is destined to be disclosed for us. . . (Rom. 8:17–18)

In suffering we see the closest link between God's glory and ours. Paul expresses a similar sentiment to the Corinthians: 'The temporary, light burden of our hardships is earning us for ever an utterly incomparable, eternal weight of glory' (2 Cor. 4:17). The temporary light burden is what he refers to earlier as being 'subjected to every kind of hardship . . . pursued . . . knocked down . . . continually being handed over to death' (vv. 8–10). What would for most of us be unendurable is a mere trifle to Paul, in comparison with the glory he expects to know in the future.

Peter, too, tells his readers:

> . . . in so far as you share in the sufferings of Christ, be glad, so that you may enjoy a much greater gladness when his glory is revealed. If you are insulted for bearing Christ's name, blessed are you, for on you rests the Spirit of God, the Spirit of glory. (1 Pet. 4:13–14; cf. 1 Pet. 2:20)

The marvellous truth is that, just as we are intended to glorify God, so God intends to glorify us. He does it in our lifetime, for if we reflect God's glory we cannot help but shine with his glory. All the people I have mentioned have achieved glory for themselves by living for God's glory. While we are in this world it will probably not feel much like glory; we are so much aware of our short-comings and our pain. But in the next life God will glorify us completely, and without any pain, frustration, or sorrow to dull our joy. As Peter put it, the chief shepherd will give us 'the unfading crown of glory' (1 Pet. 5:4).

We cannot imagine what heaven will be like, for it is completely beyond our experience of this world. The Bible uses images which would have conveyed the idea of splendour and luxury to first-century Christians: a city with gates of pearl and streets paved with gold, walls made of precious stones and a sea of crystal. These images would have recalled the golden days when Israel was at the height of its power and wealth, when David and Solomon were king and gold and precious stones were brought from far away to build palace and temple. They tend to mean a great deal less to us. But the Bible also speaks of a city where it is always light, where there is nothing evil, where we are in the presence of God for ever, and he heals our hurts with tenderness. We can identify more readily with that.

If harps, crowns and floating round on fluffy clouds do not motivate us to endure in this life, we can think of whatever is most beautiful and valuable to us, and multi-ply it to a factor of ten. Adrian Plass has his hero imagin-ing heaven to be like scoring a century at Lord's. I imagine it to be like the Yorkshire Dales, with good weather, music by Mozart, wine, wonderful food, and good friends to share it with — all at once!

But surely we cannot just go around imagining heaven to be whatever we want it to be? I think we can, if our imagination belongs to God. All we are told of heaven is by analogy with something in this world which was special to New Testament Christians. Surely parts of the creation which are special to us can have a place in heaven too? We know that the creation which has been subject to frustration will be redeemed, that it will be 'brought into the same glorious freedom as the children of God' (Rom. 8:21). I do not believe that any good thing in this world will be lost; when God makes the world anew we will find all the things we love there, but without their flaws. I fully expect my dog to be there . . . but in heaven he'll come when he's called and he won't steal my chocolate!

God who made the world and called it good, who lived in it, yearns over it, and works for its perfection, will one day fulfil his plans for our happiness. Then our pain, our faults and our limitations will drop away from us. Then we will fully understand, even as we are fully understood. Then we will know what glory is — and will revel in it for ever.

Night slipped to dawn and pain merged into beauty,
Bright grew the road his faithful feet had trod;
He gave his salutation to the morning
And found himself before the throne of God.[4]

4

In the Presence of his People

*The evening started with choruses, led by one of those
people who Gerald says have 'A' levels in Ecstasy.
All very enjoyable until someone went up to the front
and whispered something into the ecstatic fellow's ear.
When she'd finished, he spoke to us in one of those
close-to-the-microphone voices.*

*'That sister has shared with me her feeling that the
Lord is saying there are folk here who are not released
in physical expression of their joy. He would have
them know the joy of true freedom in worship.'*

*Adopted my expression of prayerful calm concern
. . . Gerald . . . leaned over and whispered in my ear.
'We'll find that "sister" afterwards, and duff her up,
shall we?'[1]*

One rainy afternoon a couple of years ago there was a
matinee film on television which had a lot to say about
worship — and it didn't even mention God. It was a true
story about an Australian racehorse called Pharlap. When
he arrived at the trainer's stables Pharlap was ugly, under-
weight, and had warts on his face. As if that wasn't bad
enough, he also lacked the will to win races. But despite
all Pharlap's woeful shortcomings, his trainer and stableboy both had a hunch that he could be a winner. For
over a year they befriended him, fed him, exercised him
and trained him. In response to their love and attention

Pharlap gained weight, became fit — and still didn't win races. So the trainer and stableboy adopted an even more gruelling training routine. Then they worked on his motivation, trying to give him the incentive to win. And it paid off. Pharlap won the Australian Derby, then race after race. A riveting tale — but what has a racehorse got to do with worship?

The trainer and stableboy loved that horse with all their heart and soul and strength and mind. In other words, they worshipped him. They certainly loved him with all their hearts – their devotion was obvious. The stable lad even slept in Pharlap's stall! They loved him with their souls, their intuition. They had a hunch this horse was great, and acted on it. They loved him with their minds; they thought out a strategy for his training very carefully. And they loved him with their strength — they invested enormous amounts of energy in him. Pharlap was the most important thing in their lives, their focus.

That is the kind of attitude God wants us to have towards him. He wants us to invest everything we have in loving him — to love him passionately, imaginatively, thoughtfully, actively. That is worship — the investment of our whole self into something we believe in and are committed to. We might associate worship with experiences of being ecstatic or embarrassed, blissful or bored. Almost certainly we associate it with church or with conferences. For many people worship has acquired an even narrower definition. It has come to mean singing a particular kind of song, written in the last five or ten years, and sung in a medley of similar songs. I've attended many services where hymns of praise have been sung, the congregation has joined in a liturgy extolling the wonders of God and his salvation, and then the leader has said, 'Now we'll have a time of worship'!

But this is much too limited a view. The whole of the service is worship. More than that, the whole of life is worship, if we really belong utterly to God. St Paul exhorts us to 'offer your bodies as living sacrifices . . . *which is your spiritual worship*' (Rom. 12:1 *NIV*, italics mine). If we have presented our bodies as a living sacrifice to God, then the whole of our daily grind becomes spiritual worship in God's eyes. Winning contracts, attending committees, washing up, singing praise songs; everything is done to the glory of God.

If, on the other hand, that love for God isn't there, then we aren't worshipping no matter how many or how 'anointed' the worship songs we sing. It isn't the type of song, the presence or absence of liturgy or the service format that matters. The Bible tells us again and again that God is more interested in our motives and our attitudes than in the outward observances of worship:

> Truly, obedience is better than sacrifice, submissiveness than the fat of rams. (1 Sam. 15:22)

> Sacrifice gives you no pleasure, burnt offering you do not desire. Sacrifice to God is a broken spirit, a broken, contrite heart you never scorn. (Ps. 51:16–17)

> To do what is upright and just is more pleasing to Yahweh than sacrifice. (Prov. 21:3)

> Faithful love is what pleases me, not sacrifice; knowledge of God, not burnt offerings. (Hos. 6:6, quoted by Jesus in Matt. 9:13)

It was because of his faith that Abel offered God a

better sacrifice than Cain, and for that he was
acknowledged as upright when God himself made
acknowledgment of his offerings. (Heb. 11:4)

With what shall I enter Yahweh's presence and bow
down before God All-high? . . . You have already
been told what is right and what Yahweh wants of you.
Only this, to do what is right, to love loyalty and to
walk humbly with your God. (Micah 6:6, 8)

If you are bringing your offering to the altar and there
remember that your brother has something against you,
leave your offering there before the altar, go and be
reconciled with your brother first, and then come back
and present your offering. (Matt 5:23–24)

Some would dismiss the Old Testament quotations as
concerning mainly the sacrificial system, which is no
longer relevant to us. But sacrifice was merely the normal
form of worship in the Old Testament, and the same
principle behind these verses applies to other expressions
of worship:

Alas for you, scribes and Pharisees, you hypocrites!
You pay your tithe of mint and dill and cummin and
have neglected the weightier matters of the Law —
justice, mercy, good faith! These you should have prac-
tised, those not neglected. (Matt. 23:23; cf. Luke 11:42)

Note that none of these biblical writers is saying that
our worship must be accompanied by the appropriate
emotions. Rather, they are saying that our worship is
unacceptable unless our daily lives give practical proof of
godly attitudes. Such proof is found not in religious activi-

ties but in the honesty and kindness with which we treat others, and in our concern for justice. Too often we in the renewal movement are concerned with having the 'right' emotions during public worship rather than the right behaviour when worship is over. Adrian Snell recorded a song which highlights the irony of this situation.

Hey, glory hallelujah
there's a lot of people singing
and I think I get the message 'bout really being free
all this holding hands and saying you're gonna love
   each other,
all this talk of Jesus
but you didn't talk to me.[2]

True worship is our whole self committed to God, and the lifestyle which results from God's love working through us. But of course the nature of our public, corporate worship also matters enormously. My ideas about God and about how I should live were very much influenced by the hymns and songs sung when I was a child. Unfortunately the words we sang often fell short of the truth, and as a result I suffered both spiritually and emotionally. The hymns were stirring – but they depicted an ideal rather than the reality. I was left with feelings of guilt and failure, and I suspect that I was not alone.

In worship as in teaching there is bound to be a gap between the ideal and the real. We strive for a standard we have not reached; we have a vision which is not yet realized. That's fine as long as we try to be honest about the whole thing. We need to make it clear we are describing an ideal. The problem with some of the hymns we sang was that they gave the impression they described an actuality. 'Every day with Jesus is sweeter than the day before' — try singing that to Jeremiah! We all have off days . . . even the saints and the prophets.

We are in danger of discouraging those who already have a low opinion of themselves. Perhaps even worse is the danger of deceiving ourselves into believing our experience to be better than it actually is. If we sing it often enough we come to believe it — even if it isn't true! Or we can switch off from worship because the gap between what we are saying or singing and our own experience becomes too uncomfortable. Ultimately this has a deadening effect on us. It will also put off outsiders who witness our worship, because they will know it to be false. Clearly it is important, both for the health of ourselves and our churches and for the sake of our witness, that we get our worship right. And that's not mainly a matter of the right technique or the right songs.

Honest worship needs to spring out of our hearts and our lives. So often there is a big gap between what we sing and what we do or think. Joseph Bayly, the American humourist, pointed out the gap between reality and hymnody. He suggested more honest versions of some famous hymns:

'Amazing grace, how sweet the sound/that saved a wretch like you.'

'Jesus, I am resting, resting, resting, resting, resting, rest. . .'

'The church's one foundation/is tax-deductible'

When morning gilds the skies, my heart awaking cries
Oh no, another day!'[3]

We might find it easy to laugh at the golden oldies. But
many people have expressed to me a similar unease about
some of our more modern songs. How can I sing 'I just
want to praise you' when I'm feeling depressed? How can
I sing 'My heart's one desire is to be holy' when I have
a strong desire to get married/own my own home/be pro-
moted? In fact, it is possible to have in the same service
several songs which talk about 'my one desire' — with
each song's desire being different! Are we thinking about
what we sing? Do we really mean it? Does it matter?
One worshipper recently told me that it doesn't, 'because
when you're worshipping you're usually thinking about
something else anyway'. Certainly we should avoid going
on a guilt trip about every lapse of attention or every
emotional swing. But at a fundamental level our worship
should reflect the truth — the truth about God and about
us.

I think this is what Jesus meant when he told the
Samaritan woman that:

A time is coming and has now come when the true
worshippers will worship the Father in spirit and truth,
for they are the kind of worshippers the Father seeks.
God is Spirit, and his worshippers must worship in
spirit and in truth. (John 4:23–24, *NIV*)

It is not where we worship that matters, whether conse-
crated or unconsecrated, nor the particular form of liturgy. What matters is that we have God's Spirit within
us, and so are 'in the Spirit' as we worship. Our spirit

must be in tune with God's Spirit; we must literally 'enter into the Spirit of' the worship. Some years ago I read an ecclesiastical dignitary's description of worship at his cathedral:

> We are very proud of our magnificent worship. We like to think that if, when the liturgy is proceeding and the choir are singing, the cathedral roof should roll back and Almighty God appear with all the hosts of heaven, we should carry on without a pause.

That cannot be worship in the Spirit, which is about communication with God. If you are talking to a loved one on their mobile phone and they surprise you by walking in the door while you are still speaking, you don't carry on as if nothing has happened. It is the person, not the telephone, who is the focus of your conversation. But in worship we often concentrate so hard on the telephone that we forget about God being on the other end. And that can happen whatever our preferred style of worship.

Worship in the Spirit is open to all Christians, no matter what our tradition. It depends solely on our having the Spirit of God within us and allowing him to do his work. All Christians have the Spirit of God (see Eph. 1:13), but we have a responsibility to allow ourselves to be filled continually with the Spirit. And true worship will be the result:

> Be filled with the Spirit. Sing psalms and hymns and inspired songs among yourselves, singing and chanting to the Lord in your hearts, always and everywhere giving thanks to God who is our Father in the name of our Lord Jesus Christ. (Eph. 5:18–20)

Just as our own efforts to be good are fruitless unless we have the righteousness of Christ, so our own efforts to worship worthily are failures unless we have God's Spirit. Having the Spirit, the outward form of worship becomes less important; it is the substance and the spirit of it that matter. If a child draws you a picture or writes you a poem, you are not disappointed because he's not Michelangelo or Keats! You're just pleased that the one you love has expressed love for you. If we love God he will be pleased with what we do by way of worship, even if it is imperfect.

Nevertheless, the content of our worship is still very important. We are to worship not just in spirit, but 'in spirit and in truth'. Jesus told the woman, 'You [Samaritans] worship what you do not know; we worship what we do know' (John 4:22). It is vital that we know who we are worshipping and what he is like. I am suspicious of the genuineness of any worship that does not lead to a hunger for knowledge about God, and of any supposed movement of the Spirit that does not give a central place to good biblical teaching. How can we worship a God whom we do not know? And however much we think we already know, there is always far more about him to be learned.

Polish doesn't matter, nor place, nor form. But truth does matter. God is truth, and our worship must be true; it must tell the truth about God. It is good to have songs which express in simple words what we feel towards God. But Romans 12:2 tells us that it is by the renewing of our *minds* that we are transformed. Worship that does not engage and stretch our minds is unlikely to change our lives in any lasting way.

What then? I shall pray with the spirit, but I shall pray with the mind as well: I shall sing praises with the spirit and I shall sing praises with the mind as well. (1 Cor. 14:15)

As Terry Virgo said when preaching at a Wimber conference:

If I want to praise my milkman I don't go around saying, 'Praise the milkman!' No, I tell people how reliable my milkman is, that he's always on time and the milk is good quality.

We need songs and hymns with real content; songs which raise our faith and our spirits and proclaim to everyone what a great God we worship. We need songs which actually teach us more about God as we sing. Many of our old hymns are marvellous in this respect, and Graham Kendrick has written a number of songs with solid theological content. But too many of our newer 'worship songs' are focused on our feelings about God rather than on God himself. There is certainly a place for this kind of song, but if it forms the main emphasis of our worship we are being seriously impoverished. Worse, people who don't experience warm feelings towards God, or who don't express them in that style, are excluded. And there can be many reasons for a lack of such feelings: an unemotional temperament, exhaustion, depression, bereavement, or the lack of a genuine encounter with God. Such people need to feel included and accepted in our churches and our worship; it is all too easy to alienate them.

Other people may enjoy the worship because it makes

them feel good, without its having any real connection with their daily lives. Years ago I knew an elderly man who had an only child, a grown-up unmarried daughter who was very devout and impeccably behaved. I'll never forget the day he spoke fervently of his favourite hymn – 'Where is My Wandering Boy Tonight?'! Another man, who only came to church twice a year, assured me that he loved to sing 'I'm Not Ashamed to Own My Lord or to Defend His Cause'. In more recent years I've sometimes discussed with worship leaders my concern over songs which are misleading in their doctrine. The response has usually been something like, 'I can feel the Spirit's presence when we sing that song, so I know it's all right!'

But is it the Spirit who comes when we sing those songs, or is it simply that the emotional atmosphere of the place changes? I was a teenager in the Sixties, and I can still remember how the atmosphere became emotionally charged whenever certain songs were played. 'This is the Dawning of the Age of Aquarius' produced a sense of hope, joy, and peace so real it could almost be touched. But the song was not true; it merely said what we wanted to hear and made us feel good about ourselves. Christian worship must be true.

Of course we respond to a good tune and optimistic words. But if we are to worship in truth, we must be critical of what we sing. Is it the truth about God? Us? The world? If not, it is better left unsung. Our critical faculties need to be applied not just to individual songs, but to the whole pattern of our worship. Whatever our tradition or style, we easily get into a rut. Then we find ourselves over-emphasizing one or two aspects; emotional or intellectual, rejoicing or reflection, positive or negative, old or new, structured or spontaneous. But all of

these things come from God and should be offered back
to him in worship.

The Psalms, the Jewish hymn book, give us a marvellous pattern for balanced worship. Firstly, they express
truth about God. They speak of who he is and what he
does. 'Yahweh is tenderness and pity, slow to anger, full
of faithful love. Yahweh is generous to all, his tenderness
embraces all his creatures' (Ps. 145:8–9). 'He spreads the
snow like flax, strews hoarfrost like ashes, he sends ice-
crystals like breadcrumbs, and who can withstand that
cold? When he sends his word it thaws them, when he
makes his wind blow, the waters are unstopped' (Ps.
147:16–18). 'He has rescued me from death, my eyes
from tears, and my feet from stumbling' (Ps. 116:8).

The psalms are poetry, so truth is often expressed meta-
phorically rather than scientifically: 'High above, he
pitched a tent for the sun, who comes forth from his
pavilion like a bridegroom, delights like a champion in
the course to be run' (Ps. 19:4–5). The truth here is not
expressed in factual or scientific terms, but we understand
that the psalm celebrates God's power and the goodness
of his creation. We see his goodness also in his care for
human beings, especially the helpless: 'Yahweh protects
the stranger, he sustains the orphan and the widow.
Yahweh loves the upright, but he frustrates the wicked.
Yahweh reigns for ever, your God, Zion, from age to
age' (Ps. 146:9–10).

The important thing about this kind of praise is that
you don't have to be in a good place to sing it. It remains
true no matter what the state of your emotions or your
spiritual life; and as it says nothing about your beliefs or
feelings, no dishonesty is involved in singing it. In fact,

you may learn something about God and find your faith increased.

Of course the psalms do express lots of emotion — but it's **the full range, not just the 'good' feelings**. The psalmists don't try to deny their anger, their envy, their loneliness, their despair, or even their desire for revenge. 'Hear me, O God, as I voice my complaint' (Ps. 64:1, *NIV*). 'God, you have rejected us, broken us, you were angry, come back to us!' (Ps. 60:1). 'I am like a desert-owl in the wastes, a screech-owl among ruins, I keep vigil and moan like a lone bird on a roof' (Ps. 102:6–7). 'My heart writhes within me, the terrors of death come upon me, fear and trembling overwhelm me, and shuddering grips me. . . May they recoil in disorder, may death descend on them, may they go down alive to Sheol, since evil shares their home with them' (Ps. 55:4–5, 14–15).

But these psalms do not merely wallow in self-pity or negative emotion. The psalmists, having owned up to their feelings, have allowed God to meet them where they are. They can then move on to express renewed hope, and faith in God's love and purpose for them. Psalm 73 is a good example; it expresses the frustration and envy of a man who tries to do right, and finds that the unscrupulous prosper more than he does. But having got that off his chest, he realizes the value of his relationship with God and his future glory. His perspective and sense of values is restored.

The psalms were written to be sung in public worship. Whatever your state of mind happened to be, some part of the worship would reflect it. Of course it was unlikely, then as now, that every worshipper present would share the sentiments expressed in every part of a service. The important thing was that over a period of time the Temple

worship would give a balanced view of the life of God's
people; the times of blessing, the dry spells, the miracles,
the unanswered prayer. In many of our churches the
worship is lopsided, so that a very inaccurate picture is
given of the Christian life.

We no longer share the Jewish tradition of radical honesty in public worship. We sing 'I love you, Lord, and I
lift my voice' but not 'I'm angry, Lord, and I raise my
voice'! Like Julie in the TV comedy 'Nurses', our never-
ending cheerfulness masks our inability to cope with pain
and dirt. Even the Anglican lectionary omits the angry
and vengeful verses of the psalms. Are we afraid of letting
God know that we have strong feelings? But he made us
the volatile beings that we are, and knows our every
mood. And he cares so much about us that he became
one of us, so as to understand us better.

So often we behave as if our worship has no connection
with our everyday lives; as if we are not creatures who
have bodies, homes, jobs, worries and pleasures. But the
message of the Bible is that God is prepared to be
involved, physically and emotionally, with us and our
world. The psalms turn into worship the ups and downs
of ordinary people and the nitty gritty of their lives. We
tend to miss this, because we see the Israelites as belong-
ing to a different world from ours; at the same time more
romantic and more spiritual. Yet the stuff of ordinary
human life is there: illness, bereavement, betrayal, guilt,
homesickness. They even wrote worship songs about the
Temple being smashed to pieces. We might (if we're
talented) write a song when our church is dedicated or
celebrates an anniversary — but when it's *vandalized*?
We leave our rock and folk artists to sing about the hard

times. The world has taken over a function which has largely been abandoned by God's people.

Some time ago I heard Nigel Forde read one of his 'psalms' to a large audience.

'Insufferable, the Little Children'

1. Why art thou so vexed, O my soul: and why art thou so disquieted within me?

2. Thou must be joking when thou sayest they are breaking up already: I mean, we have scarcely got through the Easter eggs.

3. O, what sins have I committed: that I am chastened as with a rod?

4. After six weeks of uninterrupted Wayne and Tracy: wormwood and gall will be as nectar and ambrosia.

5. Whither shall I go for peace and quiet: or where shall I hide me from their clamour?

6. If I climb the stairs they are there: if I go down, even to the living-room, they are there also.

7. My days are gone like a shadow: and I am withered like grass.

8. Their iniquities are more in number than the sand: so also are their sullen little friends with bellicose temperaments, too much pocket-money, hollow legs, unquenchable thirsts, fog-horn voices, dripping noses and mercilessly tardy bedtimes.

9. Wayne doth send out his voice, yea, and that a mighty voice: remove him from my sight lest I smite him upon the hip.

10. Who maketh the windows to shake: and his bedroom as a battlefield.

11. He pulleth the hair of his sister's head, and knappeth

her dolls in sunder: she therefore hath put sawdust in his Branflakes.

12. Six it is of one: yea, and half a dozen of the other.

13. Daily they say unto me: 'Mummy, what can I do next?'

14. Unto whom I sware in my wrath: and instantly regretted it.

15. They lay waste the kitchen like a whirlwind: storm and tempest fulfilling their words.

16. O, how amiable were my dwellings: and just look at them now.

17. By the washing-machine I sat down and wept: by the fridge-freezer I uttered my reproof.

18. One day in July or August: feels something like a thousand. Amen.[4]

Six hundred people rocked with mirth; some were actually weeping with laughter. Why? Nigel, a skilful comic, artfully juxtaposes archaic and modern phrases. He takes descriptions of the awesome wrath of the Almighty and applies them to the minor (but maddening) naughtiness of schoolchildren. The effect is just as funny as he intended. In fact the very idea of using the language and style of a psalm in a poem about modern domestic frustration is funny. But why should it be? The psalms were originally written out of real-life situations. Weeping by the rivers of Babylon may sound more romantic than weeping in your local launderette, but it's doubtful whether crying over the washing ever felt beautiful. Being held hostage, homesickness, racist taunts, a longing for revenge; if someone wrote a song about it today would we sing it in all our churches? Yet we have been singing Psalm 137 for centuries. It has been chanted by choirs and congregations and borrowed by composers from Verdi to Boney M — but often we've failed to connect its words with events in our lives and the world around us.

Do we really think that in the sixth century BC God inspired people to write worship songs about their trials and tribulations, but in the twentieth century he wants only what is 'spiritual' and 'positive' included in our worship? I am convinced that God still wants the whole of our selves and the whole of our lives offered in worship to him — the good as well as the bad. In our evangelism we often encourage people to come to Jesus as they are, rather than trying to be good enough to be accepted. 'Jesus wants you to come to him now, with all your sins, failures, and sorrows!', we exhort, starting another verse of 'Just As I Am'. And that's still what God wants, even after our conversion. In fact, 'Just As I Am' was not written about conversion. It was written by a mature Christian who was trying to come to terms with the frustrations of chronic ill health, and with not being able to serve God as she wanted to.

God wants us always to come to him just as we are, both corporately and publicly. There's no need to pretend, in church or out of it, that we are always full of faith and rejoicing, in charity with God and our fellow human beings. We feel hurt if our friends and family don't confide in us when things get rough; we want to be in it with them. We want them to trust us enough to know that we'll keep loving them, stand with them. God is like that for us.

In our worship as in our lives, God does not want us to pretend that we are perfect — or even good. He merely wants us to love him with all our heart, with all our mind, with all our soul and with all our strength. Why should we love God like that? Because he loves us like that — with all his heart, soul, mind and strength. He loves us with all his heart, and has made plain enough his yearning and affection for us: 'I have loved you with an everlasting love' (Jer. 31:3). He loves us with all his soul, and lavishes creativity and imagination on us. He loves us with all his mind; he planned the world in all its majesty and intricacy, giving it structure and rhythm; and he works out his plans for us. He loves us with all his strength; he gave it to the limit, to the point of exhaustion, suffering and death. God, in Jesus, spent himself utterly for us.

God made us to be his friends, to keep him company. When we distanced ourselves, he came to be with us, to be one of us, to win us back. He adopted us into his family and waits to take us to his home. That is God's love for us — total. How can our love for him be less? And when we love God truly, madly, deeply; with all our heart and soul and mind and strength, our worship will be meaningful and moving and sincere and exciting. Even when we haven't changed anything.

5

They'll Know we are Christians

We will work with each other,
yes we'll work side by side
Oh we'll work with each other,
yes we'll work side by side
And we'll guard each man's dignity
and give up all our pride
And they'll know we are Christians
by our love, by our love
Yes, they'll know we are Christians
by our love.[1]

Felt odd telling the truth in church.[2]

It was a picnic I'll never forget. I was 19 and I'd gone with a group of elderly and very earnest Christian ladies. We spent the morning looking round the streets of Rye, then took our lunch to the patch of lawn near Ypres Tower. 'Let's sing grace,' someone suggested, 'it'll be a good witness.' And a dozen or so cracked and high-pitched voices loudly joined in what seemed an eternal grace. To a teenage girl it was acutely embarrassing – but was it a good witness? What *is* a 'good witness'?

It is a phrase I've heard a lot in evangelical churches, especially when I was younger. It was used to justify everything from teetotalism to supershort haircuts for men. Some customs were encouraged in evangelical circles simply because it made us different from 'the world'. 'Christians must be seen to be different. It's a good witness.' Things which might be a 'bad witness' were discouraged: drinking alcohol, going to the movies, laughing at 'dirty' jokes, being angry or discouraged.

Of course we do need to be aware of the impression we are making on others, and we are not to accept unquestioningly the culture around us. But our concern for 'being a good witness' can so easily become a concern for what other people think. And our concern for what other people think easily becomes a preoccupation with appearances, with packaging rather than content. Nowadays we seem to be as much concerned with proving we are normal as proving we are different. We used to ban dancing and rock music simply because other people did them; now we have rock music and dancing in our church services simply because other people do them. There is a growing trend to package and target church services as if we were the market research department of a multinational. The rationale is the same as was the rationale for all those fundamentalist prohibitions — being a good witness. Yet I am concerned that the root attitude is also the same; a concern with our image. Yet God looks not on our image but on our heart.

Our evangelism is often concerned with making a good impression. I've heard Christian marches — both traditional Whitsun walks and the newer praise marches — justified on the grounds that 'they'll know there are a lot of Christians around'. But is that enough? What if a march by Moslems or atheists is bigger? That may give a bad impression of us, but does it discredit Christianity?

Worse is the subtle temptation to hide or bend the truth in order to give that good impression. We may be cheesed off with God or the Church, but to admit it would be a bad witness — so we dissemble. Sometimes, of course, that's necessary. It is not wise to wear our heart on our sleeve, to let the whole world know about every shift in our mood or every detail of our circumstances. There is nothing wrong with being a private person. But it is wrong to give the impression that we are always on top of things when we are sometimes very much underneath them. Nor is that such a good witness as we might think.

David Runcorn tells of a Christian friend of his who was keen on evangelism. He worked for a large company whose offices were open plan. Paul made a point of being friendly to everyone on his floor; he wished them all a good morning, enquired after their health and their families, remembered their birthdays, and was sympathetic when they were ill or in trouble. He had a genuine interest in people, and his behaviour was sincere enough. But the two men who shared his corner became friends, and with them Paul's behaviour was rather different. He told them the things that were going on in his life. They knew when he was happy, when he was sad, and when he was fed up with the infighting and power struggles at his church. Of course Paul was most unwise to share his church's problems with his workmates — wasn't he? But after a few years those two men were the only ones on that floor who had become Christians.

We are often exhorted to share the evangelistic zeal of the early Christians. How often are we exhorted to share their honesty? Acts seems to show a Church washing its dirty linen in public. Lying, bribery, hypocrisy, differing views, angry quarrels between leaders — these things happened publicly and were recorded for posterity. Nor was it felt that this reflected badly on God. They had always been clear that God's people fell short of God's glory — it was what God did with such material that gave him credit!

We too often think that God looks good when we look good — or perhaps that is just the way we rationalize our attempts to preserve appearances. But the Church's respectability is what puts most people off, particularly when they know or suspect that the underlying truth is different. As a teenager I was very impressed by some of our church's young people who could pray eloquently and spontaneously; then I discovered that they played strip poker in each other's gardens. It was three years before I wanted to have anything to do with God again. Our hypocrisy is probably the greatest hindrance to evangelism — yet we justify it in the name of 'being a good witness'.

I do not think this is what either God or the world wants from Christians in terms of witness. Jesus did not say, 'You are light for the world. . . Let your worship be lively and always make a positive confession.' What he said was, 'You are light for the world . . . your light must shine in people's sight, so that, seeing your good works, they may give praise to your Father in heaven' (Matt. 5:14, 16). How we behave, and whether our lives match up to our words, is crucial for our witness. Psalm 15 describes the standard expected of those who love God:

> Yahweh, who can find a home in your tent,
> who can dwell on your holy mountain?
>
> Whoever lives blamelessly,
> who acts uprightly,

who speaks the truth from the heart,
who keeps the tongue under control,

who does not wrong a comrade,
who casts no discredit on a neighbour,
who looks with scorn on the vile,
but honours those who fear Yahweh,

who stands by an oath at any cost,
who asks no interest on loans,
who takes no bribe to harm the innocent.
No one who so acts can ever be shaken.

This psalm describes a person of utter integrity; some-one whose heart and tongue are both truthful; who wrongs no one, maligns no one, yet despises the des-picable. He or she honours their commitments, even when it turns out to be to their disadvantage to do so. They refuse to take an unfair or excessive profit (nothing here about market forces!) and will not side against the innocent, even for personal gain.

All this is pretty obvious; surely it doesn't need saying again? After all, it is unlikely any of us has ever been offered a bribe to harm the innocent. Perhaps not . . . but how many of us have kept silent when the boss accused someone unfairly, simply to save our own skin or protect our promotion prospects? How many of us have failed to speak out against something wrong, because we knew it would make us unpopular? How many of us have put someone else down to make ourselves look bigger? We are all guilty.

Even worse, there is a tendency to think that 'the guidance of the Holy Spirit' justifies our lapses in integrity. I have known people 'guided' to break a commitment they had been 'guided' to make in the first place. Others are 'led by the Holy Spirit' in one direction one week, and in a different direction the next. Of course the Holy Spirit is like the wind, which blows wherever it will and cannot be tamed. But he is also the *Holy* Spirit – the Spirit who inspired the words of Psalm 15. And he has said that those who want to live with God will keep their word. According to James, the person who is 'in two minds, inconsistent in every activity', is more likely to be filled with doubt than with the Holy Spirit (Jas. 1:6–8). Nor does Paul approve of frequent changes of plan:

. . . do you think I lightly changed my mind? Or that . . . I have in my mind Yes, yes at the same time as No, no? As surely as God is trustworthy, what we say to you is not both Yes and No. The Son of God, Jesus Christ . . . was never Yes-and-no; his nature is all Yes. (2 Cor. 1:17–19)

We have rightly emphasized the personal guidance of the Holy Spirit. We must all pay attention to his promptings. But in making decisions it is unwise to rely too much on subjective impressions or the kind of coincidences which might indicate the will of God. It is easy to see a pattern where we want to see it! Years ago I became interested in a young man called John, who was also interested in me. I prayed about whether I should allow this relationship to develop, and plonked my finger at random on a verse of the Bible. It read, 'There was a man sent from God whose name was John' (John 1:6, *RSV*). For confirmation I took a card from a promise box. It read, 'Acquaint now thyself with him, and be at peace: thereby good shall come unto thee' (Job 22:21,

AV). At the time I was much impressed; this *had* to be God's will! I was disappointed when the relationship didn't last. Yet those two verses had been taken wildly out of context . . . and I had ignored the first two cards out of the promise box because they meant nothing to me. It was the third 'promise' that seemed to speak to the situation, and which I held on to. We all tend to select what is meaningful to us and ignore the rest, and we may not even be aware that we have done so. That makes circumstantial guidance very unreliable.

It is so easy to convince ourselves that God is saying whatever we want him to say. I have known church leaders decide God was guiding them to renege on a financial commitment because of a coincidence in the timing of a phone call. Some Christians even plead that God has led them to commit adultery and to abandon their children. Contrast that with the following comment from an Italian judge who devoted his life to fighting the Mafia:

I have learnt that whatever happens, you have to behave decently – to show real respect for what you believe in and not just make meaningless gestures. This harmony between one's beliefs and one's actions is crucial to our physical and mental well-being. I have learnt that every compromise – every betrayal, every time you fail to face up to something – provokes a feeling of guilt, a disturbance of the soul, an unpleasant sensation of loss and discomfort with oneself. Just as the categorical imperative of the Mafia is 'to tell the truth', this has become a cardinal principal of my own ethics, at least as far as the really important relationships in my life are concerned. However strange it may

seem, the Mafia has taught me a lesson in morality. . .
I, too, have learnt to shorten the distance between
saying and doing. . .[3]

Sometimes I wonder if charismatics have an advantage
over the Mafia . . . the anaesthetizing effect of the Holy
Spirit on an uncomfortable conscience!

But of course this is nonsense. The Spirit works in us
to make us the sort of person who can live with God; a
person of utter integrity, whose thoughts, feelings and
actions conform to the truth. God wants us to behave
honestly; to consider what is right rather than just what
suits us. He wants us to be people of our word, reliable.
God is merciful and forgives us our errors, but we owe
it to him not to make those errors a way of life. As Paul
implies, those who are called by the name of Christ must
be trustworthy. If we are not, the world to which we are
trying to witness may well conclude that God cannot be
trusted either.

A gap between teaching and practice is bitterly
resented. There was an outcry recently when a well-
known agony aunt admitted that she had not slept with
her husband for 20 years. She had been having an affair
for the same length of time, and she had recently discovered that her lover had been two-timing her. 'How
dare she advise others when her own life is in such a
mess!', was the general response. We in the Church come
in for the same kind of criticism, because our lives often
don't measure up to the claims we make. Nor is this true
only in terms of morality; we are lacking in the reality
the world is so hungry for.

When I was at theological college I occasionally filled
in for the housekeeper during her holidays. One summer

vacation we had two groups booked in; one of postgradu-
ates from New State University, the other from Paradise
College. The two groups were chalk and cheese. The New
Staters were secular, liberal, humanist and demanding.
The Paradise lot were fundamentalist Christians, politi-
cally and morally right-wing — and *nice*. The New Staters
shouted when they didn't like the service and gave standing ovations when they did. The Paradisers were always
terribly polite. And they smiled. All the time, in *every*
situation . . . but seldom with their eyes. The New Staters
invited me to sit with them at meals, to attend their
parties and to join them for drinks in their rooms. The
Paradisers gave me theological books. They were trying
so hard to be a good witness, to show that Jesus had
the answer to every problem. The New Staters were not
impressed. As far as they could see, the Paradisers didn't
know there *were* any problems in life. Or if they knew,
they were not admitting it. The Paradisers hadn't a hope
of evangelizing the New Staters because they weren't real.

It wasn't that the New Staters weren't interested in
Christianity. I found that when I drank beer with them
and showed myself willing to discuss feminism, dysfunc-
tional families, astral projection, and the limitations of
our laundry, they were quite open to hearing about my
faith. They just wanted to know that I was living in the
real world, and that I was genuinely interested in them.

By contrast, I've tried the evangelistic techniques that
seem to work for others, without getting a nibble. At one
time I always read my Bible on trains and planes, because
I'd heard of people being converted that way. Every
speaker or writer seemed to have a similar story, and it
usually went like this:

Speaker 'Last year I was flying to a speaking engagement at a big convention in Los Angeles [or London, or Sydney, or Hong Kong]. I was reading my Bible, and I could see that the man in the next seat was interested.'

Fellow Passenger 'What's that you're reading?'

Speaker 'It's the Bible.'

Fellow Passenger 'Gosh, I didn't know people still read the Bible. Can I become a Christian?'

Speaker 'It was a real privilege to lead him to the Lord on the spot. I heard from him just last week and he's really going on with the Lord, and his wife and three beautiful children have been wonderfully converted too. In September they're all going to Mount Zion Bible College, and they're hoping to serve the Lord overseas. I give all the glory to God!'

When I tried it, the results were always very different. It was obvious from the reactions of my seat partners that they just thought me a real nut . . . and probably afraid of flying into the bargain. Why else would anyone read a Bible on a plane? The problem was that I wasn't being real. I wasn't reading the Bible because I wanted to read it at that moment; I am actually a compulsive looker-out-of-windows when travelling. The Bible was just a gimmick to get their attention. Most people have a nose for insincerity like a pig has for truffles . . . only, pigs *like* truffles.

We should respect the dignity and integrity of others as well as our own. In our desire to reach people for God we sometimes forget this and resort to manipulative tactics, both in personal evangelism and in evangelistic services. I know of evangelists who plant people in the congregation who will appear to 'respond' to an appeal, to encourage others to follow suit. There are several variants of this ploy. Once some friends of mine who were attending a tent crusade were in a position to see the entire congregation. The evangelist had asked people to raise their hands if they wanted to become Christians. While the rest of the congregation bowed their heads in prayer, the man said repeatedly, 'I see that hand . . . thank you . . . I see you, sir . . . thank you, madam . . . yes, I see your hand. . .' My friends, who had irreverently kept their eyes open throughout, reported that in fact not a single hand had been raised.

It is not uncommon for those offering the laying on of hands to give a surreptitious push to those who come forward, to give the impression they have been slain in the Spirit. In fact this has been done to me, by a well-known healer who didn't know I was on the staff of the church he was visiting! Judging by the number of people I know who have had a similar experience, it must be a fairly common practice.

I have attended many evangelistic meetings where pro-longed and emotional singing has been followed by a lengthy sermon in which the emotional mood is changed frequently and abruptly. An appeal to the listeners' sympathies ('this is a fallen world. When I see those starving waifs on the news. . .') is followed by attempts to make them feel guilty ('how many of you can honestly say that you've never caused your mother a moment's anxiety?'); which in turn is followed by an attempt to produce fear ('if you were run over by a bus tonight, could you be one hundred per cent sure you would go to heaven? One young man refused to respond to my appeal last week, and the same night he died in a motorbike accident. . .'). This kind of thing may go on for an hour, and the effect is to keep the listener emotionally off balance and weaken his or her resistance to an appeal.

We denounce these as brainwashing tactics when they are used by cults — but some Christian evangelists use them too. Some techniques used in leading worship are medically defined as hypnotic: singing the same song over and over again, slightly increasing the tempo and volume each time; asking people to 'wait on God' and then suggesting what sensations they might experience; suggesting a response they might wish to make. A Christian neurologist attending one meeting in which it was claimed that 'the Spirit is at work' told me he could have obtained the same results without mentioning God at all.

I am sure that most evangelists and worship leaders using such methods are unaware that they are being manipulative. They are simply copying what they have seen others do with apparent success. This is the way they have learned to do it. But the decision to follow Christ is the most important that anyone can make, and they must be completely free in the making of it. There must be no coercion, no psychological trickery. There can be a fine line between effective preaching techniques and manipulation, and we need to know when we are in danger of crossing it. For that reason I would like to see clergy and lay ministers trained in basic crowd psychology, so that mistakes can be avoided. How can we be sure that any conversion occurring in such circumstances is genuine? Certainly the fall-out rate among those converted in evangelistic rallies is very high. And those who have once made a response under such conditions and have then fallen away are unlikely to become interested in Christianity again.

Fortunately we have gifted evangelists who do not

compromise their own integrity or their listeners'. They are effective communicators who present the truth clearly and leave people to make their own choice. We need to support and encourage them. Some of the others, however, have given evangelism a bad name. The Decade of Evangelism has generated almost as much fear as enthusiasm, and it is mostly ourselves we have to blame.

The increasing interest in New Age philosophies, Eastern religions and the occult shows a hunger for spirituality in our society. Yet people are not, on the whole, turning to the Church. We have lost our credibility, and we can't simply blame liberalism for having blunted the cutting edge of the gospel. Our lack of reality is easily identified from outside. We are God's witness in this world; if we are not real, people may well conclude that God is not real either. Therefore, if we love God and the world it is vital that we are ruthlessly honest with ourselves, individually and corporately. The early Church was amazingly open about its deficiencies and disagreements as well as its triumphs, and people were not put off; it was a growing Church.

In contrast, the life of most of our churches is shrouded in secrecy. Of course confidentiality is essential in pastoral matters and in counselling, but we extend it to corporate matters as well. Meetings of PCCs, elders and deacons; the choosing of a new minister; the selection of bishops; personality differences and disagreements between leaders: all are supposed to be confidential. Even loyal church members are often kept in the dark about matters which affect them and their church. In effect, they are prevented from reaching responsibility and maturity as a congregation . . . or are treated as if they have not. Although various reasons are given for such secretive practices, I have reached the conclusion that most of it is actually motivated by the leaders' desire to establish and protect a position of power.

> . . . the judgement is this: . . .
> people have preferred
> darkness to the light
> because their deeds were evil.
> And indeed, everybody who does wrong
> hates the light and avoids it,
> to prevent his actions
>   from being shown up;
> but whoever does the truth
> comes out into the light,
> so that what he is doing
>   may plainly appear as done in God.
>   (John 3:19–21)

There is no exclusion clause here for church leaders, either local or national, free or established. It is time that the running of our churches was brought into God's light.

This may be repugnant to our British reserve, and the results may seem messy. But we are more likely to witness to the redeeming power of Christ by showing how Christians handle difficulties and dissensions than by pretending we haven't got any. It is not as if we are fooling anyone.

One vicar I know had a blazing row with his wife one Sunday morning. Too upset to face his wife or his congregation, he flung out of the vicarage and began to walk. When he came to himself he was two miles from his church and it was already past the time for the Eucharist to begin. Deeply ashamed, he turned back. When at last he slipped into the back of the church, the lay reader was leading morning prayer. When the service finished the vicar went to the front and told the congregation that he and his wife had had a row and he had been unfit to take the service. He apologized for having let down his wife, his congregation and God. He stayed for coffee after the service . . . and no one spoke to him about the incident. They simply pretended it hadn't happened. The one exception was a non-Christian visitor. 'That,' she said, 'was the most honest thing I have ever heard in a church. I visit churches regularly, and until this morning I thought Christians were only play-acting.' We Christians like to think of ourselves as lovers of truth, but it sometimes appears that truth has very little value among us.

Our love of secrecy has far-reaching effects on our corporate life. Where there is little real information, gossip is bound to flourish. People's confidence in their leaders diminishes when they suspect they are not being told the whole truth. Nor are they likely to be enthusiastic in supporting the church and its mission when they are not consulted or even informed about its decisions. Hidden agendas and undercurrents of tension make for an uneasy atmosphere, and misunderstandings and misjudgements abound. Yet the quality of our relationships is essential to our witness. Jesus said, 'It is by your love for one another that everyone will recognize you as my disciples' (John 13:35). Yet anger, jealousy and criticism so often flourish in churches. I suspect it is because they are not owned up to and dealt with. And it shows; non-Christians are often more perceptive than we give them credit for. I know of one man who attended a single church service and said to his friend, 'This church is tired and disaffected.' It was true. Such things make our churches unattractive, and often hinder us from inviting outsiders to them.

In other ways, too, honesty is essential to our witness. We must be very careful not to make exaggerated claims about our experience, or in our teaching. They can quickly be shown to be false, and then our credibility has vanished. We trust those manufacturers who submit their product to rigorous testing; we too need to be able to demonstrate the truth of our claims. If we believe the Bible teaches something which is not yet true in our experience, then we need to say so. If we want to claim a miracle or a healing, we must be prepared to have it verified.

The evangelical Christian physician Dr Peter May has made repeated attempts to find medically attested healings, but he seems to have met no response but resentment. I find this disturbing; if God really does heal miraculously, what have we got to lose by submitting evidence? And if real miracles are rare, then we had better realize it and stop talking as if they were common. We may well believe that the medical definition of a miraculous healing is too rigorous. Nevertheless, for the sake of our credibility, we would do well to adjust our terminology. God often uses natural means to answer our prayers, and few people will quarrel with us if we claim that this is what has happened. The world will not believe the Church until it can see that the Church is transparently honest. The more transparent we are, the more clearly the light shines through us!

I want to issue a caveat here. Truth — any truth — takes time to become part of us and find an outworking in our lifestyle. In the meantime there are bound to be inconsistencies; this is not the same thing as hypocrisy.

The difference is that we are willing to confront the truth and to change. Change should start in the heart and find a natural expression in what we do, not the other way round. 'Clean the inside of cup and dish first so that it and the outside are both clean' (Matt. 23:25–26).

There are two common problems with this:

1. We can genuinely think we believe something, but find ourselves not doing it. We believe that we are saved by grace, not by works — so why do evangelicals have a strong tendency to workaholism? At one time I'd have been prepared to go to a firing squad for the doctrine of salvation by faith alone. Secretly, though, I thought my relationship with God depended on my quiet time. It was not until a major operation left me temporarily unable to read my Bible that I realized my mistake. The grace of God will underpin us if we find ourselves unable to pray. God's love for us is not affected by our ups and downs, or by our ability to achieve.

2. We sometimes do things because we think we ought to, not because we really believe in them or find them meaningful. Self-discipline is essential; we can't always do just what we feel like doing. For instance, if we believe that God is calling us to a church which is different from our own tradition, we may make a deliberate choice to adopt a style of worship which seems alien to us. That is a decision based on love and respect for other people. However, if we frequently find ourselves doing something just because we feel we ought to or because it will look right, we need to beware. Our integrity may be under threat. And if we have lost our integrity we have lost everything.

More than ever, our tortured world needs truth. Our increasingly synthetic culture needs reality. Some people will hate it and reject it; others will love it and embrace it. They deserve to have the choice, and it's up to us to give it to them. But we have first to make the choice ourselves. When we choose the truth we also choose God, and freedom, and life, and self-respect. Is the choice so hard to make?

6

Out of Darkness, Into Light

God is light, and there is no darkness in him at all.
If we say that we share in God's life
while we are living in darkness,
we are lying, because we are not living the truth.
But if we live in light,
as he is in light,
we have a share in another's life,
and the blood of Jesus, his Son,
cleanses us from all sin.

(1 John 1:5–7)

Some years ago I worked in the editorial department of a Christian publishing company. I was then a staunch nonconformist with an impeccable evangelical pedigree, a strong background in Calvinist theology, and an insider's interest in the charismatic movement. I had heard most of the great preachers of the day; I had met many great evangelical leaders; I had been discussing theology almost from the cradle; I had made my own commitment to Christ at the age of eight. One of my colleagues, Richard, had a very different background. Brought up an agnostic, he had begun to explore different faiths when he went to university to study philosophy. His search for truth had led him first to Eastern religions and Buddhism, and then into Christianity via Quakerism. At the time I knew him he had been an Anglican for several years.

One day not long before I left the company we talked about what we had learned from each other. 'What I've learned from you,' said Richard generously, 'is the importance of prayer.' 'And what I've learned from you,' I returned, 'is the importance of truth.' There was a thoughtful pause while Richard took this in. Then, 'You've always seemed so concerned for doctrinal soundness. Do you really mean you're only just discovering that truth is vital?' I had to admit, shamefacedly, that it was exactly what I meant. I was beginning to realize that my enthusiasm for right doctrine was partly due to a longing for safety and security. I was more concerned for whether an idea was 'sound' (i.e. safe), than for whether it was true. Under Richard's influence my doctrine had not changed — but I *had* begun to realize the importance of pursuing truth for its own sake.

My genuine evangelical zeal had hidden a deep-seated fear of truth. Instinctively I knew that truth can be threatening, subversive; it's not *safe*. Nor do I think I was unusual in this; it is the normal human condition. Whatever our theology or tradition, we are naturally afraid of truth and of its power to change us and our world. Our fear can only be overcome when we know in our hearts God's love for us and our love for him; perfect love banishes fear. The Holy Spirit's work of forging a deep truthfulness in us is accompanied by his work of helping us to grasp the breadth and length, the height and depth of the love of God for us. Jesus, when he came among us, was full of grace and truth. Most of us would like the grace without the truth, though we may hide our preference from ourselves.

We usually distinguish between theological truth (doctrine), moral truth (honesty), and psychological truth (reality). Yet deep within us all three mingle and are interdependent. That is why it is so important that we each make a study of biblical doctrine, maintain an honest lifestyle, and look to our emotional and psychological health. If we neglect any of these it will surely have an effect on the other two. And any refusal to face truth threatens our welfare. Dishonesty has its dangers.

When we find reality hard to cope with we tend to employ what psychologists refer to as defence mechanisms. A quick look at some of these may throw light on some of our more puzzling behaviour.

Projection: attributing to someone else attitudes, failings or conflicts that are really our own. If we are frustrated by our own disorganization, we may see others as inefficient and be irritable with them for it. If we cannot admit to our ambition or desire for power, we may think others are angling for status. And I have frequently heard men who could not cope with their own strong feelings accuse women of being emotional. All these are examples of projection.

Projection can become a deeply entrenched habit, or it can operate in specific and limited situations. Whenever I accept a new challenge or a new job, I get cold feet shortly afterwards. Can I meet the new demands that will be placed on me? What if it doesn't work out? If my confidence is at a low ebb these feelings can be particularly painful. This was the case after accepting one job that was quite different from what I had done before. I really wanted the job, however, so I tried to ignore my feelings of inadequacy.

Then I had a phone call from one of my future colleagues. When we had finished talking I was convinced that Phil thought me unsuitable for the job. I was upset and resented him for his low opinion of me; I foresaw a difficult working relationship. Eventually I discussed the incident with a friend. As we talked the incident through it became clear that Phil had said nothing whatever to indicate that he doubted my abilities. I had merely projected my own doubts and sense of inadequacy onto him, and then assumed that was his opinion of me. When I realized that those feelings belonged to me and not to him, I was able to come to terms with them. If I had continued projecting them on to Phil, I would have started work with a real chip on my shoulder which could have sabotaged our working relationship and my effectiveness in the job. As it was, he proved to be a most supportive colleague.

As in that case, projection is often linked with *reversal* — experiencing our own feelings as coming back at us from someone else. For example, we may have very strong feelings of aggression and anger which we find it difficult to admit to. We perceive the anger as directed at us by other people, and may misinterpret quite innocent actions and comments as aggressive. We may become touchy and defensive, or even violent. Or if we cannot admit to our own sexual urges we may think other people are trying to seduce us. Some of the Church Fathers were passionate men who could not come to terms with their sexuality, and saw all women as temptresses. That's one reason we hear so little of the Church Mothers!

Repression: the stifling of uncomfortable memories or feelings so that we are no longer conscious of them. These repressed feelings cause tension, drain our energy, and may cause illness or influence our behaviour in ways we are unaware of. I have known several women, models of Christian uprightness, who have repressed their sexuality.

Drab clothes, blouses buttoned to the chin, no make-up, a personality without sparkle — and their conversation is sprinkled with sexual innuendoes of which they are unaware. Another woman, who lived alone, was burgled. Outwardly she was not much shaken, and maintained that she was not afraid to be on her own in the house. It was only when she began to wet herself every time she entered the house that she admitted her fear and sought help.

Repressed emotions can be picked up by other people. I have known a friendly and relaxed group become edgy and aggressive when a person with repressed hostilities entered the room. In extreme cases repressed energies and conflicts can be transferred to material objects. Most experienced exorcists agree that poltergeist activity is usually caused not by an evil spirit but by a deeply troubled person within the house. In one case a married woman woke to find her wedding ring hanging from a tree branch outside her closed window; she turned out to be racked with guilt from an illicit love affair. In another case, a newly married woman experienced a deep conflict between the desire to spend nights with her new husband and an obligation to nurse her seriously ill mother. Sexual epithets mysteriously appeared daubed on their house and scratched into the paintwork of their car. Such problems usually respond to expert counselling, while exorcism will make little difference.

Regression: going back to an earlier stage of development, often as a response to frustration or fear. We may find ourselves with a sudden urge to cuddle soft toys, or become involved in arguments of the 'you did!' 'did not!' 'did so!' variety. There is a story about a famous naturalist who was making a TV programme about the rain forest canopy. He was winched 200 foot up into the tops of the

trees, but when the time came for him to come down
again it was found that the mechanism had failed. The
man had a guilty secret; he was afraid of heights. As he
climbed slowly and painfully down the swaying rope, he
swore savagely and vividly. The fear grew, however, as
he got further down and the rope began to swing more
violently. The great outdoorsman completed his descent
repeating plaintively: 'Mary had a little lamb. . .'. When
he finally reached the ground he found his camera crew
collapsing with laughter — his microphone had been live
throughout that traumatic descent! We may laugh too,
but in a situation of great stress or terror any of us may
respond by regressing to the behaviour or the comforts
we experienced as a child.

Turning against self is a form of *displacement:* if we
cannot cope with being angry at someone else we may
turn the anger against ourselves. There can be various
reasons for not allowing ourselves to be angry with
another. If the person is using emotional blackmail on us
we may feel guilty about our anger, not realizing it is
justified. Or if the person we are angry at is a 'victim',
perhaps ill or disabled, we may again feel guilty. It may
not be 'safe' to express anger against its real object if that
person is in a position of power over us, or if professional
etiquette prevents us from doing so. This is an occupa-
tional hazard among clergy and others in the caring
professions!

We may simply have been brought up to be uncomfortable about expressing anger. But if we do not find some
outlet for it, it may well turn in on ourselves, producing
illness, depression, self-destructive behaviour or suicide.
During that traumatic final year at university which I
described in Chapter 1, the anger that I'd been bottling

up for so many years turned into self-hatred. I literally wanted to obliterate myself, and only the grace of God kept me from doing so. For several years afterwards I refused to spend any more money on myself than was absolutely necessary, and abandoned my interest in fashion to wear dowdy clothes that didn't suit me.

For years I found it difficult to express anger to someone's face, but I learned other ways of venting it. When I was a shop assistant I kept a supply of giant bubble wrap in the store room. Whenever a difficult customer had really got on my nerves, I used to go out back and burst some bubbles. The worse the customer, the more bubbles I'd burst. That was the beginning of my efforts to find ways of expressing my anger without turning it against myself.

Denial: refusal to face an unacceptable truth. Denial is a normal stage in coming to terms with bereavement or our own impending death, but is often employed in other situations too. If there has been a shock, denial is often expressed as 'I can't believe this' or 'I just can't take it in'. The week before writing this chapter I was driving along the M62 from Manchester to Bradford when I came upon a queue of stationary traffic leading into a fog bank. There had been a multiple accident. Lorries and cars were littered over the motorway like Dinky toys in a nursery. Eventually the police waved us by, and I drove over bits of shattered taillights and car trim as I passed the wrecked vehicles. Rounding a lorry that was tilted across two lanes, I suddenly saw a car wedged partly under it. From the door protruded a woman's legs — and the door was shut. A grim-faced policeman stood with his back to the wreckage, and an unnerving silence hung over the scene. I wanted to stop the car and cry, but I had to keep moving. I passed another four accidents before arriving at my destination an hour later, a shaking heap. Nor did my condition improve much over the next couple of hours.

I commented to friends that I couldn't understand why I was taking it so hard. I had passed accident scenes before without being unduly upset. After all, I couldn't be sure anyone was hurt . . . by that time I was certain I had imagined the legs, and I didn't mention them. I also had the impression that I must have been travelling a mile or so behind the pile-up.

The evening news carried the story, announcing that one person had died. The car they showed was the one I had seen and which had affected me so powerfully. It was early the next morning before I accepted that I had probably not imagined the legs protruding from it. After all, someone *had* died in that car. Driving the route again a few days later, I found that in fact I had been travelling not far behind the wrecked vehicles. Had I not been delayed a few moments as I was leaving the house, it might have been me under that lorry. My mind had played me two tricks, a temporary form of denial. That enabled me to adjust to the shock bit by bit, instead of taking it in all at once.

It is possible to live in a permanent state of denial of events, circumstances or facets of our own personalities which we would rather not acknowledge. Children do this when they 'forget' being abused; the memories may surface years later when they are adults. Adults may deny their debt, their business problems, their guilt. Churches operate in denial when they 'forget' sick people who have not responded to prayer for healing.

In fact most defence mechanisms can operate in a

similar way within a group as within an individual. Certain facts of reality or common experience can be denied; emotions and drives can be repressed; there can be a regression to childish, dependent behaviour. If a group as a whole is denying some aspect of reality (doubts, disagreements, suffering. . .) there is a strong but subtle pressure on every member within the group to deny them too. In an individual who belongs to the group, this can lead to a conflict between what is perceived to be the truth, and loyalty to the group. If the 'forbidden' feelings or perceptions refuse to go away a person may feel guilty, or develop low self-esteem because he or she does not fit in. Some people become disillusioned with Christianity altogether, because they do not see the Church coming to grips with reality. On the other hand, the person who does conform to what the group expects may adopt the same defence mechanisms used by the group, with harmful consequences.

In churches and movements where denial and repression are common, projection is also common. Robin Skynner and John Cleese have described this process very clearly:

John Real extremists are very proud of the purity of their beliefs.

Robin Yes. Of course, there's nothing wrong with trying to improve yourself, as long as you're realistic. But the moment you try to convince others, and even try to convince yourself, that you're *purer than you actually are*, that means you've got to start screening off the bits of you that don't match your claim.

John And once they go behind the screen, they get projected onto other people or groups.

Robin Now if you're the person doing that, of course it does make *you* feel purer, more perfect — for a while.

John Just as during the Inquisition they thought they were getting high marks from God and doing Christ a good turn by burning people alive. . . Presumably the same applies to the witch-hunting in Britain in the seventeenth century. Because the Puritans felt that sexual feelings were so wicked, they all screened them off, and projected them onto other people — the poor old 'witches'.

Robin That's right. Then if they did have improper sexual thoughts themselves, they could blame the witches for putting these into their minds.[1]

Nowadays we don't hold an Inquisition or burn witches. Instead we may over-emphasize the demonic and spiritual warfare; every misfortune and every failing is the devil's work. We do not lust or feel discouraged; we 'have an unclean spirit' or 'a spirit of oppression'. Ministry to such 'spirits' may produce a quick result, but it will be a temporary one. The real problem is our failure to take responsibility for ourselves and face up to what we are. This in turn may be due to a failure to realize the depth of God's love for us just as we are.

I believe that evil spirits do exist and sometimes trouble people, but that this is relatively uncommon. Some charismatic groups emphasize the occult to the extent that they exist in an atmosphere of superstition, living in fear of the evil powers. For years I frequently 'prayed for protection' and 'put on the armour' as I had been told to do. I tried to foresee every possibility of something going wrong, so that I could ask God to take care of it. I became increasingly uncomfortable with this practice, however. The underlying rationale seemed to be that the devil was always near, always aware of my activities, always waiting to get in if I relaxed my guard. God, on the other hand, was further away and less aware of what was going on in my life – or perhaps less likely to take the initiative. Why else would I need to ask specifically for his protection in every eventuality? Now I know there is no need to live in fear, for the God who loves me is much more closely involved in my life than the devil is.

In psychological terms, my acute awareness of the devil had sprung from my inability to cope with the evil inside me — I had projected it onto spiritual entities outside myself. Moreover, this was the norm in the group of which I was a member. The group as a whole projected evil onto the spirit world. In other groups the evil will be projected onto human beings. This is one reason why some Christian groups become very sectarian, thinking everyone who disagrees with them is wrong, out of God's will, or even evil. Tension can develop over quite small differences of doctrine or practice, with the motives of the 'opponents' being grossly misunderstood. The unacceptable traits of one group are being projected onto the other, who are then treated as the enemy.

This is often what lies behind religious militancy, and it explains why groups at the extremes of churchmanship keep splitting. The concern for purity of belief and practice shown by the members of these groups is a reflection of their inability to cope with their own impurity. They need to keep finding a new 'enemy' in order to keep justifying themselves. Skynner and Cleese describe the process in terms of political parties; they identify 44 extreme leftist groups and 20 extreme rightist groups. The splintering process is an ongoing one, however, and new groups are forming continually.

The same phenomenon occurs with religious groups. A group which leaves an existing church is more than likely to split again within a few years. I knew one housegroup which left a denominational church, only to split twice more within three years. And those who have left the Episcopal Church in the USA over the issue of women's ordination have not been able to agree well enough to form one cohesive denomination. No wonder the New Testament views schism so seriously.

We may genuinely believe we are combatting evil by picketing the shrine of Our Lady at Walsingham, or by marching to drive out evil spirits and claim ground for Jesus. But the chances are that we are actually running away from the sin that we know to be in ourselves, and are afraid to confront. Jesus did not show much sympathy with this attitude; his consistent teaching is that we are to allow God to deal with our own sin rather than concerning ourselves with the sin of others.

There is probably little we can do to change the Church, except to change ourselves. We can try to be more honest, and to encourage others to be honest too. It is important that we do so, for corporate dishonesty does nothing either for the welfare of individual members or for the credibility of the group as a whole. By becoming real people ourselves, we will help create an atmosphere in which other people can be real too. People who have admitted their frailty and been rejected or put down will hesitate to do so again; we can affirm them and encourage them.

Often defence mechanisms are ways of coping that we have learned as children, especially if our childhood was difficult. They may have been the best way to survive emotionally then, or simply the way of coping which we learned from our parents. They help us to deal with an uncomfortable reality while ensuring our survival emotionally and psychologically. They become a problem when we get so stuck in them that we do not realize the situation is different, or that we have changed. In other words, we may become so used to functioning in a given way that we do not realize it is no longer appropriate. We may begin using defence mechanisms not as a way of coping with reality, but as a way of avoiding it altogether. When we take this to extremes our mental health may be threatened. The psychiatrist Scott Peck says:

> In *The Road Less Travelled* I defined mental health as 'an ongoing process of dedication to reality at all costs'. Satan is utterly dedicated to opposing that process. In fact, the best definition I have for Satan is that it is *a real spirit of unreality*.[2]

This is not to say that mental illness is sin. Mental illness, like any other illness, may strike people who have done nothing to deserve it. Nevertheless, our mental and spiritual health are at risk if we allow ourselves to become out of tune with reality. We employ defence mechanisms when we want to avoid facing the truth. But God is truth, and when we turn away from truth we turn away from God. If we are out of touch with reality, we are out of touch with God. He *is* reality. And if we hide the things we are ashamed of, afraid of, or which cause us pain, we prevent God's love from reaching and healing us. 'Though the light has come into the world people have preferred darkness to the light because their deeds were evil' (John 3:19). Yet God knows all about us and loves us anyway; '. . . it is proof of God's own love for us, that Christ died for us while we were still sinners' (Rom. 5:8). Jesus, having shared our human nature, can sympathize with us in all our weaknesses and our sufferings.

God knows us inside and out, both our past and our future, and we are secure in his hands. Therefore we can pray,

> God, examine me and know my heart
> test me and know my concerns.
> Make sure that I am not on my way to ruin,
> and guide me on the road of eternity.
>
> (Ps. 139:23–24)

In fact God constantly exerts on us a gentle but ruthless pressure to face the truth and live by it. Often he will allow the pressures of life to build up to a point where our hidden weaknesses are exposed and can be dealt with. This is one reason why suffering often becomes a growth point. But if we resist the process we are stuck with our problems and may become worse.

For many of us, hiding from the truth of ourselves has become such a habit that we don't know how to do anything else. How then do we learn to walk in the light? Slowly and cautiously! The first step is, as always, to pray about it. We might use the words of Psalm 139, or Psalm 43:3: 'Send out your light and your truth; they shall be my guide.' Adrian Snell has recorded a song I sometimes use as a prayer:

> Many times I've been smiling
> When inside I've been crying,

I've been shaking hands with people
Who just didn't know my pain.

Many times I've been walking
When inside I've been running,
I've been standing in the sunshine
But could only feel the rain.

Lord, I'm weary
I've got nothing more to hide,
And I've had my share of turning
Turning with the tide.

Many times I've been winning
When inside I was losing —
Well, I liked to hear the cheering
But it didn't ease my mind.

Many times I've been leaving
When inside I was staying,
Often wished the road before me
Was the one I left behind.

Lord, I'm weary
That is why my head is bowed,
And I've had my share of running
Running with the crowd.

I've had my share of reaching out
But never really touching,
Lord, let me feel the healing touch
Of Jesus in my soul.

I've had my share of crying out
But never really praying —

> Lord, I want to say I'm sorry, will you
> Come and make me whole.
>
> Many times I was loving
> But inside I was hating,
> And I didn't know the reason
> Nor who should take the blame.
>
> There were times when I was looking
> But I just wasn't finding,
> I was hearing all the answers
> But the questions still remained.
>
> Lord, I'm weary
> There was nothing left to find,
> And I've had my share of blowing
> Blowing in the wind.[3]

Or we can simply say to God in our own words that we would like to become more honest and more truthful; if we suspect that there is something we're not facing we can admit it and ask for courage. God will lead us in the way which is right for us, showing us the things which he would like to deal with and wants us to face. There is usually no need to go through an orgy of introspection; God can bring issues to our attention one at a time. It is the decision to face truth rather than running away from it that is important; we have a lifetime for truth to become more and more a part of us.

But how, practically, does that happen? Are there ways in which we can co-operate with God as he brings things to our attention? Here are some suggestions:

1. If you are emotionally repressed and stifle your feelings, you will need to make a conscious effort to identify

your emotions. As soon as you feel something, however faint, stop and centre in on it. If you are used to shutting down on your feelings, this will be very difficult at first — especially as there will probably be a time lag between the event and the reaction. It has taken me 15 years to reduce my reaction time from years to minutes, and to identify my reactions reasonably accurately. You may well make more rapid progress!

Beware the temptation to reason yourself out of whatever you are feeling; you feel what you feel. Identify your emotion and find a safe way of venting it; only then can you know whether or not it is legitimate. It may be useful to listen to music which expresses feelings similar to yours. This will help you to stay with your mood rather than running away from it. *Don't* use music which runs counter to your mood to try to alter it. God help me, I have even used worship LPs to try to escape from the reality of my circumstances and my feelings. As if the adoration of God, who is truth, can be used to escape the truth!

2. Try keeping a journal. If you can be sure that no one else will read it, you will be free to express thoughts and feelings that would otherwise be bottled up. It may help to address them directly to God, in a written prayer or a letter. Writing things down is often a tremendous relief; we can get things off our chest that we wouldn't want to say to another person. The act of writing forces us to identify our thoughts and feelings more precisely and to put them into some kind of order, so that they stop whirling about in our brains.

3. As the inner you becomes released you may be overwhelmed by strong feelings. Try making an offering of them to God. Anger, frustration, confusion, doubt,

loneliness: what a lousy offering to bring the Eternal
King! But, incredibly, it is the sort of offering he wants;
'sacrifice to God is a broken spirit' (Ps. 51:17). Jesus died
so that we can exchange our weak and flawed personalities for his strong and wholesome one. It's an exchange
that goes on all our lives, if we co-operate, and which he
always welcomes with joy. But it must be a genuine offering, a complete relinquishment. He may lift these things
from us or not, as he chooses. But now they belong to
him, he is *in* them — and that changes everything.

You might try performing some kind of symbolic
action. Often our instincts tell us what this should be. At
one time when my life seemed in darkness and confusion,
I had a sudden impulse to take my shell collection out of
the box it had been stored in for some years and put it
on display. I worked for a couple of hours, unwrapping
seashells from yellowed newspaper and arranging them
carefully on shelves in a display cabinet. I felt that what
I was doing was very important, but I didn't know why.
When I'd finished, I knew — and I made it a prayer.
'Lord,' I said, 'I want you to do with me what I've just
done with these shells; take me out of darkness into light,
and put my life into order.' Immediately I felt much
better.

4. Pay attention to your dreams; dreams often give us a
clue to what is going on inside ourselves. They are the
voice of the Holy Spirit working in our inner self, alerting
us to the neglected parts of ourselves and to factors we
are overlooking. Therefore, if we want to be honest with
ourselves we will do well to try to understand what our
dreams are telling us. At first we may need help from
someone who is skilled in working with dreams; as dreams
contain messages we are trying not to hear, an outsider's

objectivity is very helpful. With practice we will probably be able to understand them without help. It is worth the effort; dreams are one of the Holy Spirit's ways of bringing our darkness into God's light. I spent several months working on my dreams with a Jungian therapist, and it was an experience of real spiritual growth.

For instance, I once dreamt that I was taking my dog for a walk round a town square. The square was lined with walnut trees, and as we walked Alfie ate a fallen walnut. The police promptly arrested me and imprisoned me on a charge of giving civic property to my dog. I spent the afternoon in the town jail, but towards evening I got fed up and walked out of prison. It was not until I recorded the dream the next day that I realized the walls of my cell had simply been painted on the floor; I had stayed inside the lines voluntarily. The dream was telling me that I had an over-sensitive conscience which was treating trivial offences as if they were serious. I was in a prison of my own making, and the time had come to walk away from it. That dream was liberating.

5. Read the kind of books which will help you to increase in self-awareness. Good, easy-to-read books on mental health abound. They might be Christian, such as John White's *The Masks of Melancholy* or *Eros Defiled*; or Scott Peck's *The Road Less Travelled* or *People of the Lie*. Both men are experienced psychiatrists writing with spiritual insight. Secular books can be equally helpful. *Families and How to Survive Them*, by Robin Skynner and John Cleese, describes the stages of our psychological development and what happens if we are blocked along the way. It even has cartoons! Or there are books for specific problems, such as Robin Norwood's *Women Who Love Too Much*. This describes the relationship

difficulties faced by women who have had an unbalanced family life, and gives advice on how to overcome them. The Bibliography and Notes contain information on these and other books. I consider it an important part of my pastoral ministry to keep a selection of such books for loaning out.

Classic literature can also make healthy reading. Novels, biographies and poetry may all help us to increase in self-knowledge. Good novels and biographies, in particular, are concerned with the development of character. They can teach us much about ourselves. On the other hand, it is wise to treat devotional books with caution while we are going through this process; they so often deal with the ideal rather than the real.

6. Facing up to the hidden things is often easier with the help of another person — a friend, spouse, listener, pastor or trained counsellor. In time you will learn to recognize whether a particular problem just needs a listening ear or whether you could do with some trained help. The Acorn Christian Healing Trust has a network of trained listeners.[4]

It might be helpful to see a therapist. Many Christians are suspicious of psychologists and psychiatrists, thinking that their faith will be undermined. But good therapists are trained to respect the client's beliefs and values. Their aim is to help the person become truly themselves, not to change their belief system. Nor is therapy only for those with acute mental problems; every therapist must receive therapy themselves in the course of their training. Therapy is simply a useful tool towards self-knowledge and personal growth.

And self-knowledge is not an optional extra for the Christian. It is essential if we want to grow closer to God and more like him. We can only effectively give to God what we know of ourselves; what remains unknown also remains unsanctified. God wants and deserves to have all of us — including the bits we're uncomfortable with. God wants us to bring our whole self, including our dark side, into his light. And when we draw near to God, then he will draw near to us.

> I've had my share of reaching out
> But never really touching,
> Lord, let me feel the healing touch
> Of Jesus in my soul.
>
> I've had my share of crying out
> But never really praying —
> Lord, I want to say I'm sorry, will you
> Come and make me whole.[5]

Notes

Chapter 1 Truth from the Heart

1. Jane Austen, *Emma*.

Chapter 2 The Shadow of the Almighty

1. J. H. Sammis, 'Trust and Obey' from *Hymns of Faith*. London, Scripture Union, 1964.
2. Author unknown.
3. C. Austin Miles, 'I Walk in the Garden Alone'.
4. 'Every Day with Jesus is Sweeter than the Day Before': I have not been able to discover the author or publisher of this song.
5. J. H. Sammis, 'Trust and Obey', op. cit.
6. St Teresa of Avila, *The Interior Castle*, tr. Halcyon Backhouse. London, Hodder & Stoughton, 1988, pp. 121–2.
7. Ibid., p. 30.
8. C. H. Spurgeon, *Lectures to My Students*, First Series. London, Marshall, Morgan & Scott, no date, pp. 178–9. A one-volume paperback edition is now available from the same publishers.
9. M. Scott Peck, *People of the Lie*. London, Arrow Books ed, 1990, p. 123.

Chapter 3 Glory!

1. Anne Ross Cousin, 'The Sands of Time Are Sinking' from *Methodist Hymn Book*. London, Novello, 1933.
2. Bono, 'I Still Haven't Found What I'm Looking For' from

U2's LP 'Joshua Tree'. UK copyright held by Blue Mountain Music Ltd.

3. Robert Browning, 'Andrea del Sarto' from *Browning: A Selection* by W. E. Williams. Harmondsworth, Penguin, 1954, pp. 209–10.

4. Author unknown.

Chapter 4 *In the Presence of his People*

1. Adrian Plass, *The Sacred Diary of Adrian Plass*. Basingstoke, Marshall Pickering, 1987, pp. 83–4.

2. Phil Thomson, 'That's Me in the Corner', from Adrian Snell's LP 'Listen to the Peace'.

3. Joseph Bayly, *Out of My Mind*. Wheaton, Illinois, Tyndale House Publishers, 1970, p. 109.

4. Nigel Forde, 'Insufferable, the Little Children' from *Fluffy Dice*. London, Robson Books, 1987.

Chapter 5 *They'll Know we are Christians*

1. Author unknown.

2. *The Sacred Diary of Adrian Plass*, op. cit., p. 118.

3. Judge Giovanni Falcone with Marcelle Padovani, tr. Edward Farrelly, *Men of Honour: The Truth About the Mafia*. Fourth Estate, 1992. I have quoted from an extract published in *The Sunday Times*, 6 Sept. 1992.

Chapter 6 *Out of Darkness, Into Light*

1. Robin Skynner and John Cleese, *Families and How to Survive Them*. London, Methuen, this edition 1993, p. 136.

2. *People of the Lie*, op. cit., p. 207.

3. Phil Thomson, 'Prayer' from Adrian Snell's LP 'Something New Under the Sun', lyrics copyright Thank You Music.

4. Known, logically enough, as Christian Listeners. For more information contact The Acorn Christian Healing Trust,

Whitehill Chase, High Street, Bordon, Hants., GU35 0AP.
Tel. (0420) 478121/472779.
5. Phil Thomson, op. cit.

Bibliography

If you would like to explore further some of the topics I have raised, you may find the following books interesting. This is a small selection of the many good books available, and I have not listed here any titles already found in the Notes.

NORWOOD, Robin, *Women Who Love Too Much*. New York, Pocket Books, 1985. Now available in the UK. For women who frequently find themselves in unhealthy or non-reciprocal relationships.

PARKER, Russ, *Healing Dreams*. London, SPCK, 1988. Guidelines on how to understand your dreams and find in them a resource for growth.

PECK, M. Scott, *The Road Less Travelled*. London, Arrow Books, 1983. Suggests ways in which facing our difficulties can enable us to reach a higher level of self-understanding.

PIPPERT, Rebecca Manley, *Hope Has Its Reasons*. London, Collins, 1990. Facing what is really wrong with us . . . and finding hope in God's love.

ROSE, Lynda, *No Other Gods*. London, Spire Books, 1990. The difference between Eastern and Christian meditation, drawing on pre-conversion experience of TM and on Christian classics on spirituality. Suggestions for Bible-based and Christ-centred meditative prayer.

SANFORD, John, *Dreams: God's Forgotten Language*. New York, Harper & Row, 1990; distributed in the UK by Harper-Collins. Understanding how God speaks to us through dreams, from a Jungian perspective.

SANFORD, John, *Healing and Wholeness*. New York, Paulist

Press, 1977; available in the UK. A look at Christian healing, drawing on many sources including Jungian thought.

TOWNSEND, Anne, *Faith Without Pretending*. London, Hodder & Stoughton, 1990. Well-known conservative evangelical painfully realizes that life and faith are not as simple as she had thought.

WHITE, John, *Changing on the Inside*. Guildford, Eagle, 1991. The relationship between repentance and emotional health, and the possibility of real change.

WHITE, John, *Eros Defiled*. Leicester, InterVarsity Press, 1977. Help for Christians in coming to terms with their sexuality.

WHITE, John, *The Masks of Melancholy*. Leicester, InterVarsity Press, 1982. The many masks of depression; why Christians get depressed; forms of therapy available. Primarily for friends, relatives, pastors and counsellors of the depressed.